# Employment Law for Early Years & Childcare Providers

## IMOGEN EDMUNDS

Copyright © 2023 Imogen Edmunds

All Rights Reserved. No part of this publication may be reproduced, stored in or introduced into any retrieval system, or transmitted, in any form, or by any means (electronic, mechanical, photocopying, recording or otherwise) without the prior written permission of the author.

The author specifically disclaims any liability, loss or risk which is incurred consequently, directly, or indirectly, of the use and application of any contents of this work. This book is not a substitute for legal advice, which should always be sought by the reader.

This book is sold subject to the condition that it shall not, by way of trade or otherwise, be lent, resold, hired out, or otherwise circulated without the author's prior consent in any form of binding or cover other than in which it is published and without a similar condition including this condition being imposed on the subsequent purchaser. Statutory pay rates quoted are current as of 1st August 2023.

# DEDICATION

To 'Team Redwing' for always delivering our core values. You are all superstars!

# Contents

Why do Day Nurseries, Pre-schools and Out of School Clubs need this book? ............................. 9

Those pesky acronyms… ................................. 13

Introduction- "Why is employment law so blinkin' difficult?" .............................................. 15

Safer Recruitment ........................................... 21

Do I have to provide a reference to an ex-employee? ........................................................ 25

Avoiding discrimination in recruitment ........... 31

Enhanced Disclosure from DBS ........................ 32

Age Discrimination and Pay ............................. 35

Sex and Gender discrimination ........................ 35

The risk of Health or Medical Questionnaires . 38

Responsibilities of the employer to report if they have concerns to the Disclosure and Barring Service (DBS) in England & Wales ....... 41

Probationary Periods ....................................... 44

Pay ..................................................................... 48

National Minimum Wage ................................. 51

"How can I avoid the pitfalls of National Minimum Wage?" .......................................... 55

Contracts of Employment ................................. 61

What do Early Years and Childcare Employers need to consider with their Written Statements? ..................................................... 64

Pensions ........................................................... 65

Allegations against employees ......................... 66

The Fair Process .............................................. 67

Pregnancy and Maternity ................................ 69

What happens with benefits during maternity leave? ............................................................... 73

Sharing Maternity Leave ................................. 75

Supporting your employees with their IVF journey ............................................................. 78

Holiday & Leave .............................................. 82

Contracts of employment ............................... 84

Time off for Family Emergencies .................... 86

Time off for personal appointments ............... 88

What about time off to attend appointments with a partner? .................................................92

Adoption Leave ................................................94

Does an employee have any rights when they become foster parents? .....................................97

Flexible Working .............................................99

Menopause ....................................................104

Absence..........................................................107

Handling a Short-Term Absence issue ...........111

What happens when someone wants to leave? ...................................................................113

Do I have to give sick pay to my employee who has had elective or cosmetic surgery?...........116

Baby Sitting ....................................................120

Training ..........................................................124

Whistleblowing ..............................................127

Compassionate Leave ....................................129

Supporting a bereaved employee with their religious observance ......................................133

What are contractual disciplinary, capability and grievance procedures?....................................136

Can I anonymise witness statements?...........137

What happens in a disciplinary hearing?.......140

Who can be an employee's companion to a disciplinary hearing? ......................................142

When should you allow an employee to be accompanied by someone different? ............144

What happens if they resign and go sick? .....147

What if they resign with no notice?...............148

What if they don't contact you? ....................155

Retirement......................................................156

Redundancy ...................................................158

Transfer of Undertaking (Protection of Employment) Regulations aka TUPE..............161

Providing Employee Liability Information in a Transfer...........................................................166

What happens with holidays when a TUPE occurs?...........................................................168

How does a share sale differ from a TUPE transfer?........................................................170

Short Service ...................................173

So can I just write to her and dismiss?".........176

Appendix ........................................183

Checklist for Handling Grievances under ACAS Code of Practice ..............................192

Another book by Imogen Edmunds, Chartered FCIPD ..............................................195

About the Author ............................196

# Why do Day Nurseries, Pre-schools and Out of School Clubs need this book?

I didn't think I would ever write this book.

Having previously wrote a 40,000-word book in 2016 called How to Hire Superstars for your Day Nursery I can assure you I was in no hurry to write my second book!

Finding the time to write is the challenge. I love writing and have lots to say but setting aside time to 'get a book out' is the hard bit.

In my company Redwing Solutions, we are lucky enough to work with Day Nurseries, Pre-schools and Out of School Clubs every day. We are a HR Consultancy that specialises in HR for Early Years and Childcare. We hear about the challenges these employers face navigating the minefield that is employment law. It is this that motivated me to write this book. I wanted each Day Nursery, Pre-school or Out of School

Club in the UK to be able to access the information they need for under £10.

We often speak to Early Years and Childcare employers who are in what my Mum would've have described as in a "right pickle".

Often this is because they didn't know what the law required, or they didn't take the time to find out.

People can be very reactive individuals and if I had a £ for every time someone had said to me...

"So, I asked him to leave there and then".

I would be very wealthy indeed.

It's also true to say that most of the Early Years and Childcare employers in the UK are what I describe as heart-led businesses. They make decisions for their business on what is best for an employee or a customer. They care too much.

They are good people; they just don't always establish the law before acting. That's where we step in. As HR Consultants our job is to ensure that our clients act within employment law, whilst at the same time doing what is right for the business.

We help our clients to understand what is happening to provide them with options as to what they can do to address the issue they are experiencing.

Early Years and Childcare employers can have additional pressures compared to other businesses. These include:

1. This is a regulated industry. Most of the Early Years and Childcare businesses in the UK are regulated by either Ofsted, Care Inspectorate or CIW (Care Inspectorate Wales). In simple terms this means that the regulator can determine whether they are able to operate their business. They can literally 'lock the gate!'
2. They receive funding from the local authority which requires compliance and rules to be followed.

3. There is a recruitment crisis in the sector. Low pay and a requirement of high levels of skills means that there is a shortage of qualified staff to work in Early Years and Childcare. The profession is underfunded and often, sadly, undervalued.
4. These businesses are often not businesses. They are often not for profit, social enterprises and charities, trying to operate within their sector for their values rather than for profit.
5. They can be operated by parents. Still there are many Pre-schools that are committee run providers where every September a new committee is elected to run the unincorporated establishment. These committees are the employers and are often made up of reluctant parents and ex-parents who serve on the committee because they do not want to see the Pre-school close.

# Those pesky acronyms...

Every Early Years book has them and this book is no different. Therefore, before we really get into the juicy contents, I thought I would share what these acronyms used in this book mean so you can breeze through the words with ease!

| Acronym | Stands for... |
| --- | --- |
| CSP | Company or Contractual Sick Pay |
| DBS | Disclosure and Barring Service |
| EAP | Employee Assistance Programme |
| LEL | Lower Earnings Level |
| LA | Local Authority |
| LADO | Local Authority Designated Officer |
| SMP | Statutory Maternity Pay |
| SAP | Statutory Adoption Pay |
| SPBL | Statutory Paid Bereavement Leave |

SSP — Statutory Sick Pay

NMW — National Minimum Wage

## Introduction- "Why is employment law so blinkin' difficult?"

Employment law doesn't always set out to be difficult, but it can certainly be said that small employers can find it difficult to meet the expectations of law makers.

In the UK, our laws come from acts of parliament, European regulations enacted in the UK (not for much longer!) and case law.

Employers will find that in most cases, that the law is the same regardless of whether they employ 1 person or 100,000 people.

The cost of compliance has become greater over recent years and the penalties for non-compliance are becoming more severe.

We find that in Early Years and Childcare the employers have an expectation that they will need to comply with certain external requirements.

Afterall Early Years and Childcare as I have previously said is a regulated sector. In

England we have the Early Years Foundation Stage which sets out the framework within which children under 5 will experience their early education. Compliance with the EYFS is a requirement of the sector, established by the regulator Ofsted.

In that respect understanding that others will have a view on your activity as an employer doesn't come to a surprise to employers in Early Years and Childcare in the way it can with shopkeepers and cleaning companies for example.

Most employers we speak to are very familiar with the requirements of operating a childcare business but less familiar, and as is often the case, therefore less comfortable with the requirements of employment law.

I guess this makes sense. I can't tell you how to change a nappy in a way that meets the expectations of infection control, but I can tell you how many days of consultation there will be in a collective redundancy involving 20 or more employees!

If you aren't around employment law every day, navigating its requirements can seem like an overwhelming difficult ask.

In some cases, the fact that Early Years and Childcare operations are sometimes incredibly small it can make it more of a challenge to comply with employment law.

Let's take the example of a small employer who is trying to investigate an alleged misconduct episode in the workplace. The ACAS guide to carrying out a workplace investigation assumes that all employers will be able to access sufficiently qualified and experienced individuals to be able to have separate people involved in the investigation stage than any future disciplinary stage.

In a small business that can be nigh on impossible. In some consultancies that will be an bone of contention and we often hear tales of employers being told that they must hire an external HR consultant (i.e. one of their consultants) in order to conduct a fair and robust process.

That can be true, but equally a guide is just a guide and is not the LAW, and a small employer can't be expected to do something that is beyond its means.

It should be carefully evaluated and if no other option exists then the same people will be able to conduct both the investigation and any disciplinary process.

Having said all of that, some laws are obvious and compliance by all sizes of employers makes sense. These include that there is no minimum workplace temperature in the UK (places of work differ so much to make it impossible to fix on a number below which employees shouldn't be asked to work) and that no worker should suffer discrimination in the workplace.

The areas of employment law that we find Early Years and Childcare employers must be knowledgeable on include the following:

- Avoiding discrimination in recruitment and selection
- Pay

- Sickness Absence
- Pregnancy and Maternity
- Holiday and Leave
- Flexible Working
- Time off for Family Emergencies
- Contracts of Employment & Written Statements of Terms and Conditions
- Transfer of Undertakings (TUPE)
- References
- Whistleblowing
- Resignations
- Redundancy
- Retirement
- Dismissals
- Disciplinary & Grievances
- Pensions
- Training

It is for this reason that you will find all these topics covered in this book.

They are the most common reason why Day Nurseries, Pre-schools and Out of School Clubs will call our HR Consultancy asking for help.

They trouble experienced employers and those managers in their first few weeks in their role in equal measure.

They are the areas of employment law that aren't for the fainthearted but are important and necessary for Early Years & Childcare employers to understand.

So, let's get started and so that it makes sense for you dear reader we have broken this book down into 3 sections of the employment journey:

- The Beginning of the Relationship
- The Bit in the Middle
- The End of the Relationship

Whilst we are talking about asking someone to leave, Early Years and Childcare employers should always ensure they use probationary periods and reserve the right to terminate employment/withdraw a job offer due to failure to provide original certificates demonstrating qualifications and for failure of the employer to obtain two references that are satisfactory to the employer.

Let's look at each of these in turn...

## Safer Recruitment

Recruiting is the practice of telling others you have vacancies. Selection is the process of deciding whom to recruit. In Early Years and Childcare, you will see much written about Safer Recruitment. In HR terms we would stress the importance of Safer Selection.

For us Safer Recruitment is an important process that ensures that individuals who work with children are suitable, qualified, and safe to do so. It involves thorough background checks, including DBS checks, and robust vetting procedures to prevent unsuitable individuals from working with children.

We would encourage employers in Early Years and Childcare to consider a Safer Recruitment Policy. This might include your organisation's commitment to:

- safeguarding and protecting all children and young people by

- implementing robust safer recruitment practices.
- identifying and rejecting applicants who are unsuitable to work with children.
- responding to concerns about the suitability of applicants during the recruitment process.
- responding to concerns about the suitability of employees and volunteers once they have begun their role.
- ensuring all new staff and volunteers participate in an induction which includes child protection.
- a list of the supporting procedures that accompany the policy.
- the date the policy comes into force and when you will review it.

Below is what must be included in your safer recruitment procedure.

- Carry out an up-to-date Enhanced DBS check or establish that the DBS is clear on the DBS Update Service.

- Make sure no one awaiting the DBS works with children alone, ideally doesn't start till the check has been undertaken.
- Use application forms rather than CVs to demonstrate safer recruitment.
- Keep notes from interviews to show you followed a robust recruitment and selection process.
- Obtain a minimum of 2 up to date references and retain these. Ask questions of the candidate if a reference can't be provided.
- Early Years providers must keep records of all people working including volunteers and students who have regular contact with children.
- Checks and copies of professional's qualifications. Remember people have and will produce fake qualification certificates and will believe they are qualified when in reality all they have is what we call 'units towards'.

- A check to see if person has right to work in the UK.

Remember during any Ofsted inspection, an Ofsted inspector will look at safer recruitment procedures and ensuring the right steps are in place to safeguard children. If you've not taken up references expect to be found out. Whilst no requirement to have a single central record, they can be useful. An inspector will often ask to see the record of a new starter and ask the Manager to take them through what happened that was Safer Recruitment.

Safer recruitment doesn't stop at the hiring decision. Are all new employees being given a full induction process specifying safeguarding and child protection responsibilities and procedures that are to be followed? This is essential. It is everyone's responsibility to safeguard children and we find new starters can often be the ones to spot a practice that has become ingrained in the culture without the employer realising it.

# Do I have to provide a reference to an ex-employee?

In short no, but it will often depend on what you have done for others. Additionally, any employer is likely to draw what we call 'negative inference' from a refusal to provide a reference.

When an employee leaves the employer should keep personnel files for 6 years post-employment. If during that period, a new employer requests a reference then so long as a record exists a reference can be provided. Even after 6 years it may be possible to advise on date started, date employment ended and job title.

Such 'scant' information is often met with dismay but is still a reference and can be used to validate the information provided. For example, if the candidate tells you they have been a Deputy Manager and the reference comes back as Early Years Practitioner at least you can challenge this.

The reason we say that the requirement to provide a reference depends on what you have done for others is two-fold:

1. References are required by the regulator and form part of Safer Recruitment, however there is no legal requirement to provide a reference in Early Years and Childcare. By contrast employers in financial services who are regulated by FCA are required in law to provide references for certain roles.
2. If everyone receives a reference and then you decide not to give one for Fred as you parted on not the best terms, you open the door for Fred to accuse you of acting in bad faith and may suggest you have discriminated by your refusal. Remember you can be accused of discrimination post-employment where Fred has a protected characteristic. Furthermore, tribunals have been won based on victimisation where the employer has been accused of deliberately refusing a

reference because the employee accused the employer of discrimination.

So, what's this bad reference malarky?

The idea that you can't provide a bad reference can cause confusion. You can provide a reference that reads badly or is negative so long as it is true. You can't provide a misleading reference that is inaccurate and says something about the ex-employee which is unknown to them.

Here's an example of what you can add in a pre-employment reference that may be read badly:

1. Fred has had 67 days of sickness absence since 1st January 2023.

Here's an example of what would be a 'bad reference'.

1. Fred would have been sacked if he had not resigned.

You have an obligation to the ex-employee to make sure you provide an accurate reference. Mess up on the data you provide, and not only might the ex-employee fail to secure their new role, but they might seek compensation from you for your failure in your duty of care towards them.

You also have a duty towards the new employer. Ever had that reference come back that was too good to be true? What might be described as 'simply glowing'. Employers must give references that are accurate, not misleading, true and fair. Otherwise, the new employer might be able to sue the ex-employer for their failure in their duty of care towards them.

It is not uncommon for ex-employees for whom you have provided a reference to ask to see it. Normally this is because their prospective employer has withdrawn their job offer.

There is an exemption under sch.2 to the Data Protection Act 2018 that allows employers to refuse to disclose a confidential employment reference to an employee or former employee.

Employers should bear in mind that the exemption under sch.2 applies only where the reference is provided in confidence. Therefore, if the employer providing the reference does not wish the reference to be disclosed to the employee, it should ensure that it is addressed to a specified person and marked as confidential.

Where an employee or former employee requests to see a reference, the employer that received the reference may decide to disclose it regardless of the exemption under sch.2, although it should exercise caution as such a disclosure may undermine relations with the employer that provided the reference.

If the employer decides to disclose the reference, it should take care not to disclose information about a third party, for example the line manager who gave the reference, unless that individual has provided their consent to such a disclosure.

If the third party has not consented, or refuses to consent, the employer may decide to disclose only the parts of the reference that do not reveal the identity of the author, for example by redacting the author's name.

References are never part of an employment tribunal judgement, and it is for this reason that employees will often seek a reference when conciliating with ACAS through the COT3 process. An agreed reference cannot be deviated from otherwise, the employer will be in breach of contract and can be sued.

My top tips regarding references include:

1. Never accept an employment reference from a Gmail account or similar.
2. Make sure staff know who is authorised to provide references. For example, don't allow Room Leaders to provide references for those in their room on behalf of the employer.
3. Mark all references provided as confidential.
4. If in doubt as to whether an ex-employee wants, you to provide a

reference obtain their written consent first.
5. Do not give verbal references.
6. Provide your own reference rather than respond to a form provided.

# Avoiding discrimination in recruitment

When it comes to recruitment and selection in your Early Years and Childcare setting the employer is responsible to make sure that all recruitment and selection is fair. The employer must ensure that no discriminatory practices have been allowed to develop in the organisation.

In terms of the stages of recruitment, there are many potential areas where discriminatory practice could creep in. Here's a list of the stages and risks associated with those stages.

- Job advertising: The language used in job advertisements should be inclusive and avoid language that may deter

candidates from applying based on their gender, age, race, religion, marital status, pregnancy, or disability.
- Shortlisting: The criteria used for shortlisting candidates should be objective and relevant to the job requirements. Avoid making assumptions.
- Interviewing: Interviewers should ask questions that are job-related and avoid asking personal questions that could lead to discrimination.
- References: References should be sought from all candidates as part of Safer Recruitment.
- Job offer: Job offers should be handled consistently and the offer made should not discriminate on the grounds of any of the protected characteristics.

# Enhanced Disclosure from DBS

Under the Rehabilitation of Offenders Act 1974, there are exceptions that allow employers in Early Years and Childcare to request to see the candidate's criminal records checks. In Scotland these will be known as PVG and in England and Wales these will be DBS. These exceptions are as follows:

- Jobs involving work with children: If the job involves working with children, the employer has a legal obligation to request an enhanced DBS check. This check includes a search for both spent and unspent convictions, cautions, warnings, and reprimands.
- Certain offences: Some offences are always disclosed on an enhanced DBS check, regardless of when they were committed. These include offences involving sexual activity with children or vulnerable adults, and certain violent or drug-related offences.

One option to avoid the cost of enhanced disclosures is to participate in the DBS Update Service. The DBS Update Service is an online subscription service that allows individuals to keep their DBS certificates up-to-date and share them with employers. It also removes the need for individuals to apply for new DBS certificates each time they change jobs or roles.

Candidates in childcare who have had a DBS check carried out can join the DBS Update Service within 30 days of the certificate being issued. This is their only opportunity to join and they cannot join retrospectively without obtaining a new DBS. To join the service, candidates need their DBS certificate number and their personal details, including their name, date of birth, and address.

To sign up for the DBS Update Service, candidates can visit the DBS website and follow the instructions on the 'Join the Update Service' page. The service costs £13 per year and can be paid for using a debit or credit card.

Once a candidate has joined the DBS Update Service, they can choose to share their DBS certificate with any employer who is registered with the service. This means that if the candidate changes jobs or roles, they do not need to apply for a new DBS certificate, if their new employer is also registered with the service.

## Age Discrimination and Pay

We often get asked why if age discrimination is a risk can employers pay employees in Early Years and Childcare different rates of pay due to their age under the National Minimum Wage. This is because the age parameters are set by the National Minimum Wage and not by the employer. Once you come away from the National Minimum Wage you are at risk of a claim of discrimination on the grounds of age.

## Sex and Gender discrimination

So, what do we mean by sex and gender discrimination and how can we avoid the pitfalls of managing staff who express their views.

Firstly, should we be talking about this at all? The recent decision that a woman who said people cannot change their biological sex was discriminated against by her employers, has thrown into sharp relief the difference between biology and gender.

Maya Forstater did not have her contract renewed after posting a series of tweets about gender and sex.

In 2019, an Employment Tribunal judge decided such views were not "worthy of respect in a democratic society".

But in a 2021 an Employment Appeal Tribunal judge ruled "gender-critical" views were protected under the Equality Act 2010. The ruling sends out a signal that employers and organisations should think carefully when deciding how to treat staff, based on their views about sex-based rights and gender identity. It also shows how divisive and difficult it can be to negotiate these conversations.

So, what does the law mean when talking about these issues? Discrimination based on belief – there is a need for employers and employees to respect the views of others even though they may not be "in tune" with the prevailing thinking on a given matter as the Tribunal upheld that Maya Forstater had been directly discriminated against because of her beliefs.

Sex discrimination – The Act protects both men and women against discrimination on the grounds of their sex, for example paying women less than men for doing the same job. Let's not forget that men can be discriminated against too.

Gender discrimination – more accurately called gender re-assignment discrimination and the Act offers protection where people who propose to start to or have completed a process to change their gender less favourably e.g., because they are absent from work for this reason.

Therefore, it is important that we all remember that we just can't cancel people and their beliefs if reasonably expressed just they are contrary to what people feel is acceptable of "right."

And that while we use words flexibly and often use sex and gender interchangeably, they often in law have very specific meaning.

## The risk of Health or Medical Questionnaires

When hiring someone to work in Early years and Childcare, it is important to ensure that the employer complies with the Equality Act 2010.

This law aims to prevent discrimination against individuals based on certain protected characteristics, such as disability, age, and gender. One area where employers may unintentionally discriminate is in the use of pre-employment medical questionnaires.

A pre-employment medical questionnaire is a document that asks job candidates about their medical history, including any disabilities or health conditions they may have. The purpose of the questionnaire is to help employers assess whether a candidate is able to carry out the duties of the job and to identify any adjustments that may need to be made to support them.

However, the use of pre-employment medical questionnaires can be risky under the Equality Act 2010. This is because they can lead to discrimination against individuals with disabilities or health conditions.

Firstly, asking candidates to disclose their disabilities or health conditions **before** a job offer is made can result in them being unfairly screened out of the recruitment process. This is because employers may make assumptions about a candidate's ability to carry out the job based on their health status, without considering any adjustments that could be made to support them.

Secondly, pre-employment medical questionnaires can be seen as a breach of privacy and may discourage individuals with disabilities from applying for jobs. This is because candidates may feel that they will be discriminated against if they disclose their health status, or that their personal information will be shared with others.

Under the Equality Act 2010, employers are only allowed to ask candidates about their health or disabilities **after a** job offer has been made. This is to ensure that candidates are assessed on their ability to carry out the job, rather than their health status. Employers are also required to make reasonable adjustments to support candidates with disabilities or health conditions, such as providing extra training or equipment.

In summary, using a pre-employment medical questionnaire when hiring someone to work in early years and childcare can be risky under the Equality Act 2010. Employers should only ask candidates about their health or disabilities after a job offer has been made and should make reasonable adjustments to support candidates with disabilities or health conditions. By following these guidelines, employers can ensure that they are not discriminating against candidates and are creating an inclusive and diverse workplace.

Staff medication is referred to in the Statutory Framework Early Years Foundation Stage. Under 3.19. Staff members must not be under the influence of alcohol or any other substance which may affect their ability to care for children. If a staff member is taking medication which may affect their ability to care for children, the staff member should seek medical advice. Providers must ensure that staff members only work directly with children if medical advice confirms that the medication is unlikely to impair that staff member's ability to look after children properly. All medication on the premises must be securely stored, and out of reach of children, always.

## Responsibilities of the employer to report if they have concerns to the Disclosure and Barring Service (DBS) in England & Wales

Early Years and Childcare employers have a legal responsibility to ensure that the people they employ to work with children are suitable, qualified, and safe to do so. As part of this responsibility, employers must report any concerns they have about an employee's suitability to the Disclosure and Barring Service (DBS).

If a Early Years and Childcare employer has concerns about an employee's suitability to work with children, they must report these concerns to the DBS. This is known as making a referral. Employers can make a referral to the DBS if they have concerns that an employee has:

- Behaved in a way that has harmed a child or vulnerable adult, or may have harmed a child or vulnerable adult.
- Behaved in a way that indicates they may pose a risk of harm to children or vulnerable adults.
- Behaved in a way that suggests they may have committed a criminal offence that would make them unsuitable to work with children or vulnerable adults.

- Employers must make a referral to the DBS as soon as possible after they become aware of the concerns. Referrals should be made in writing and include as much information as possible about the concerns, including the nature of the concerns, any relevant dates or incidents, and any action taken by the employer in response to the concerns.

It is important to note that making a referral to the DBS does not necessarily mean that the individual will be barred from working with children or vulnerable adults. The DBS will carry out an investigation and make a decision based on the information available to them.

Childcare employers must ensure that they have policies and procedures in place for dealing with concerns about an employee's suitability to work with children. This should include a clear process for making referrals to the DBS and for managing the employee while the investigation is ongoing. This will be often known as the Managing Allegations about Staff Policy.

## Probationary Periods

Probationary periods can be a useful tool for employers when hiring new employees. Here are some reasons why:

1. Assess Job Fit: Probationary periods give employers an opportunity to assess whether a new hire is a good fit for the position and the company culture.
2. Evaluate Performance: During the probationary period, employers can evaluate the employee's performance and determine whether they are meeting the expectations set out for them.
3. Identify Training Needs: Employers can use the probationary period to identify any training needs the employee may have and provide them

with the necessary resources to improve their skills.
4. Protect Against Liability: Probationary periods can help protect employers from potential legal liability by allowing them to terminate an employee who is not a good fit before they become a permanent employee.
5. Encourage Accountability: Employees on probationary periods are more likely to take their job seriously and be accountable for their actions, knowing that their performance is being closely monitored.
6. Reduce Turnover: Using probationary periods can help reduce turnover by ensuring that new hires are a good fit for the position and the company culture before they become permanent employees.
7. Flexibility: Probationary periods can be used to give employers flexibility when hiring new employees. They can try out a new hire and determine

whether they are a good fit before making a long-term commitment.

Probationary periods are not a requirement of employment law but are in fact a human resource mechanism used to try to establish that the employment gets off to a positive start.

The most common probationary period will be six months in duration. This will be less where there is a fixed term contract of less than 6 months in duration, such as might be used in a maternity cover.

During the probationary period there is an expectation that the employer will have sat down with employee and reviewed their performance in the probationary period. We recommend that these progress checks will have happened at these intervals, 1 month, 3 months and then 6 months.

It can be hard to justify a dismissal at the end of a probationary period if the employee has had no feedback in their first 6 months, or even worse, if their feedback has been incredibly positive. One of the worse things an employer can do is be contradictory. In employment, the left hand needs to know what the right hand is doing.

The employer has a few choices in the probationary period. These will include:

1. Extend the probationary period (typically for another 3 months)
2. End the probationary period and support the employee to only improve their performance.
3. End the employee's employment in the probationary period.
4. Successfully pass the employee's probationary period.

Where an employee has their probationary period extended it is very important to write to the employee and outline that their probationary period has been extended and by how long. A copy of this letter is then placed on the personnel file for future reference. It is not uncommon for employee's notice periods to increase following successful completion of a probationary period. No employer wants to be in a position where they believe they have extended and employee's probationary period, but they cannot evidence this.

Let's consider why? Well for an employee in a position of trust, a dismissal for breach of safeguarding is likely to make it impossible to secure new employment. An employee could be barred from working with children if the Disclosure and Barring Service in England and Wales determine that the employee is no longer suitable for working with children. They could therefore find themselves unable to earn a living in the profession they have trained for, and in this case if they feel unfairly dismissed are likely to look for a way to clear their name.

## Pay

Employees have several rights relating to pay which are worth a mention in this book.

1. Employees have a right to a pay statement. Its fine for this to be

emailed. It should breakdown pay received and any deductions.
2. Employees have the right to receive the National Minimum Wage and to complain if they do not without being dismissed because of it.
3. Contracts should state when pay rates are reviewed with no guarantee this will result in any increase.
4. Employers who work in the public sector will often have their pay negotiated by collective bargaining.
5. Deductions from pay will be limited to those in the contract of employment.
6. Employees can't be asked to pay for PPE.

Pay is a bone of contention for many employers. They want to be able to pay their employees more money but the impact that an increase in pay can have on other costs makes this unaffordable. If you consider that for every £10 spent on wages, you will have £3 of additional national insurance, pension costs etc you will not be far off. This 30% additional costs can help you evaluate what you can afford to do with wages.

Since the Equality Act 2010 employees are free to discuss their pay with their work colleagues and employers are forbidden from requiring employees to maintain their confidentiality when it comes to matters of pay.

Employees should expect that they will receive Equal Pay. Employers will face claims of discrimination if it is found that they have not paid women the same as men performing the same role.

When it comes to Equal Pay of Equal Value it becomes more complicated. This refers to situations where an employee will complain that they perform a role that is functionally the same to a colleague but not the same role. Back in 2012, Birmingham City Council announced it would have to find £752 million to settle equal pay claims brought mostly by women who occupied female dominated roles such as Teaching Assistants.

# National Minimum Wage

The National Minimum Wage (NMW) is a legal requirement for employers to pay their workers a minimum hourly wage. It was introduced in the United Kingdom in 1999 by the Labour government, and it remains in force today.

The introduction of the NMW was a response to concerns about low pay and poverty among workers in the UK. Prior to its introduction, there was no legal requirement for employers to pay a minimum wage, and many workers were paid very low wages, especially in industries such as hospitality, retail, and social care.

The NMW was designed to ensure that all workers, regardless of their occupation or industry, are paid a minimum wage that reflects the cost of living in the UK. It is intended to prevent exploitation and help to reduce poverty among low-paid workers.

The introduction of the NMW was initially controversial, with some business groups arguing that it would lead to job losses and damage the economy. However, these fears have not been borne out, and the NMW has been successful in raising wages for low-paid workers without causing significant job losses or harming the economy.

The NMW is now set and reviewed annually by the Low Pay Commission, an independent body made up of representatives from business, trade unions, and academia.

Employers who fail to pay the NMW can face financial penalties and other enforcement measures, so it is important that Early Years and Childcare employers comply with these regulations.

Each year since 2013, the government publishes a list of employers who have breached the NMW each year. Here are some examples of high-profile employers who have been named and shamed in recent years:

1. Sports Direct - In 2017, the company was found to have failed to pay the NMW to workers at its Shirebrook warehouse and was named and shamed by the government. The company was also criticized for its use of zero-hours contracts and poor working conditions.

2. Tesco - In 2018, Tesco was named and shamed for failing to pay the NMW to thousands of workers who were paid less than the legal minimum. The company subsequently paid out millions of pounds in back pay to affected workers.

3. Wagamama - In 2018, the restaurant chain was named and shamed for failing to pay the NMW to staff who were required to attend unpaid staff meetings. The company subsequently apologized and agreed to pay affected staff the back pay they were owed.

4. Marriott Hotels - In 2019, Marriott Hotels was named and shamed for failing to pay the NMW to over 200 employees, who were found to have been underpaid by around £71,000 in total. The company subsequently apologized and paid the affected workers the back pay they were owed.

5. Amazon - In 2020, Amazon was named and shamed for failing to pay the NMW to workers who were required to undergo security checks at the end of their shifts. The company subsequently changed its policy to ensure that workers are paid for this time.

These examples highlight the importance of employers complying with NMW regulations to avoid reputational damage and the financial penalties.

# "How can I avoid the pitfalls of National Minimum Wage?"

Early Years and Childcare employer need to be very familiar with the requirements of the National Minimum Wage. It is a fact that many employers in the sector will not be able to provide their employees with wages that are much above the National Minimum Wage.

When we consider how to encourage an employer to ensure they comply with the National Minimum Wage we often talk about the importance of diarising key birthdays that will change an employee's rate of pay. These actions are often actions you can schedule once and then relax, safe in the knowledge that you will have given yourself a task to review that employee's pay. Many employers use payroll software which will also question you before payroll is run if they think that the employee's date of birth means their salary will be below the National Minimum Wage in that pay reference period.

Where an apprentice is hired who is over 19 years of age and in their first year of an apprenticeship, they cannot be paid the National Minimum Wage for an apprentice for longer than 12 months. In that case it is the date of start that needs to be diarised. Once they have been employed for over 12 months and are over 19 years of age, they will be entitled to receive the National Minimum Wage for their age.

Another huge pitfall with the National Minimum Wage is failing to understand what you can and cannot deduct from an employee. Certain deductions impact the National Minimum Wage and certain do not. As a rule of thumb if the deduction benefits the employer, it is not allowed to take the employee below the National Minimum Wage. It is for this reason that employees who receive the National Minimum Wage or similar cannot take part in salary sacrifice schemes such as Cycle to Work.

Employers can't deduct for mandatory training such as Paediatric First Aid or

Safeguarding. These courses have to be paid for by the employer, they have to pay an employee for their time to complete these courses and cannot deduct this from the employee's wages if they leave, where such deduction takes the employee below the National Minimum Wage.

Another area that Early Years and Childcare employers must consider is whether they are requiring their employees to purchase uniform. If an employee buys uniform and this takes them below the National Minimum| Wage, then this will represent a breach of the National Minimum Wage.

Every year the employers who have failed to pay the National Minimum Wage whether this was intentional or not, are named and shamed online. This list can course reputational damage particularly when an entry is picked up by the press. Size of business makes no difference to whether an employer could find themselves in breach of the regulations. Both John Lewis Partnership and Wagamama have found themselves on the list of employers who have been found by the HMRC to have not paid their employees the National Minimum Wage.

Many employers will blame their accountant when something goes wrong related to pay. Sadly, as Company Directors it is you who are responsible for making sure you have paid your employees the National Minimum Wage. Accountants will often not accept any responsibility for your practices.

Here's a handy checklist for you to review against your practices as an Early Years and Childcare employer.

1. How are employees paying for childcare? This can't be through their wages as a deduction.
2. What uniform are you asking your employees to fund? Innocuously asking an employee to wear black trousers and black shoes will breach the National Minimum Wage if they have to go out and buy these from their money. One way round this is to relax all Dress Codes and replace uniform with tabards or similar, another is to

give employees an allowance every 6 months to purchase black trousers and black shoes to wear at work.

3. Are you paying your over 19-year-old apprentices the rate of their age once they have been an apprentice for 12 months?

4. Are you paying the apprentice the rate for their age if you have not immediately enrolled them on their qualification. An apprentice can only be paid the apprentice National Minimum Wage if they are enrolled with the training provider for that qualification. Where an employer decides to wait to review their performance in the probationary period before enrolling them, they must pay that apprentice the rate for their age under the National Minimum Wage regulations.

5. If you are intending to deduct for bad behaviour, such as a failure to return uniform, or for failure to return a set of door keys, have you detailed this in the

Written Statement of Terms and Conditions under Deductions.
6. Are you using Time Off in Lieu, and do you manage this to ensure that employees taken any TOIL due during the pay reference period it is owed. If you do not require it to be taken in pay reference period, it is earned there is a risk that the HMRC may find you in breach of the National Minimum Wage.

Finally, a word about childcare costs. It is not uncommon for us to hear from employer's who are frustrated that an employee has run up an overdue invoice for childcare and they want to deduct this from any final monies due.

Regardless of what is in the contract, a deduction that takes the employee below the National Minimum Wage will be unlawful. Childcare costs that remain unpaid at the end of employment should be treated the same as any bad debt.

# Contracts of Employment

In the UK, employers are legally required to provide their employees with a written statement of terms and conditions of employment. This statement should be given to the employee on or before their first day of work. It is commonly referred to as the "written statement of terms and conditions" or the "employment contract."

In Early Years and Childcare, we recommend that employers separate the written statement of terms and conditions from the letter of offer rather than combine them together. Furthermore, it's also very important to make sure that the contract has been drafted for an employer in Early Years and Childcare. All too often we hear from employers who ask us to explain why their previous HR Consultant has included such generous notice periods, or generous sick pay schemes when they can't afford to offer these to new starters.

Since April 2020 (when we were a tad busy with the C word) there has been a requirement that all written statements of terms and conditions include the following. This follows the work of the Taylor Review into Modern Working Practices and the production of what is known as The Good Work Plan.

The following should be included:

- the employer's name.
- the employee's or worker's name,
- job title or a description of work and start date.
- how much and how often an employee or worker will get paid.
- hours and days of work and if and how they may vary (also if employees or workers will have to work on Sundays,
- during the 'night period' or take overtime)
- holiday entitlement (and if that includes public holidays)
- where an employee or worker will be working and whether they might have to relocate

- if an employee or worker works in different places, where these will be and what the employer's address is
- how long a job is expected to last (and what the end date is if it's a fixed-term contract)
- how long any probation period is and what its conditions are.
- any other benefits (for example, childcare vouchers and lunch)
- obligatory training, whether this is paid for by the employer or not.
- The purpose of this document is to outline the key terms and conditions of the employment relationship, ensuring that both the employer and the employee are aware of their rights and obligations.

# What do Early Years and Childcare Employers need to consider with their Written Statements?

There are several questions that Early Years and Childcare employers should ask themselves before advertising a vacancy, these include:

- Will I be offering a fixed term contract? These differ from permanent contracts and are useful when hiring apprentices and those who are covering maternity leave.
- Will my employee be working at more than one location? If so a mobility clause will be needed.
- What benefits will be offered? Whatever goes in the advert will need to be reflected in the written statement.
- Is my employee going to be term time only or all year round?

- Have I checked that the salary to be offered covers the National Minimum Wage?
- Do I want to offer a casual or zero hours contract?
- Would the vacancy suit a fixed term zero hours contract where the employee will work hours as required by the needs of the business for a fixed period?
- Would be temporary fixed term contract suit the need for a summer vacancy?
- Is the employee going to be engaged as a worker using a Casual Workers Agreement?

## Pensions

Since the introduction of auto-enrolment we no longer have stakeholder pension schemes. Employers must set up an qualifying pension scheme that meets the requirements of the Pension Regulator. Whether your employee will be auto enrolled depends on many factors including their earnings before tax.

Employers also have obligations to provide employees with information regarding auto-enrolment and their rights.

## Allegations against employees

Allegations that an employee in Early Years and Childcare has failed to safeguard a child are always serious. Employers will be advised to seek advice from their local authority designated officer (the LADO or similar safeguarding lead in your part of UK) and ensure that they refer to the regulator if they feel something significant has occurred that needs reporting.

Where an allegation is made against an employee, worker or volunteer in Early Years and Childcare it is important to follow the procedures for reporting allegations in accordance with your own policy.

HR and Employment Law advisors will be able to support you but you need to only act on the employment side of things once you have received the 'go ahead' from the safeguarding lead.

Whilst we are on the subject we have seen a huge discrepancy between how LADO's treat allegations. Everything from LADO's who have scolded employers for not suspending the employee and seeing it as a serious case for referral and then another LADO in a different area taking the view that the exact same issue is not their concern and wondering why they had been contacted.

It is important when handling allegations made against staff that a fair process is followed. It is these situations, that if poorly handled, are going to lead the employee to claim that they have been wrongly dismissed.

## The Fair Process

Well firstly there will have been a referral to LADO or similar as we have discussed. Then once advised to continue the employer will undertake a thorough and robust investigation looking for evidence to confirm or deny the allegations. CCTV can be particularly wonderful in allegation of breaching safeguarding investigations. Statements can be taken from witnesses and the alleged employee interviewed. The employee would be if disciplined advised of the disciplinary hearing with such notice to enable them to prepare and arrange a companion. The letter calling the hearing will include all the evidence that the employer will be referring to and the hearing will take place in a good location. If it is decided to terminate the employment of the employee where the allegation is proven to the satisfaction of the employer, them the employee will receive a letter confirming their dismissal and right of appeal.

We do hear of instances where "Fred was asked to leave there and then". I always worry in those cases as to what process the Early Years and Childcare employer has followed. In the sector all employers do have a obligation to safeguard children and if employees are dismissed with notice without a fair and robust procedure, the chances are they will be employed at another setting within 72 hours.

## Pregnancy and Maternity

There's not a day that goes by where we don't hear about a new pregnancy in one of our employer's small businesses. It could be the abundance of women of childbearing age working in the childcare, it could be that working with children triggers hormones, it could be in the water. Whatever it is, we see many Day Nurseries for whom pregnancy and maternity is an area of Employment Law that they must be confident and competent over.

The Maternity Regulations 1999 are a set of UK laws that apply to pregnant women and their employers. Here are some key points to know about these regulations:

- Time off for antenatal care: Pregnant employees are entitled to paid time off

work to attend antenatal appointments, including medical check-ups, ultrasound scans, and classes.
- Maternity leave: Pregnant employees are entitled to take up to 52 weeks of maternity leave, regardless of their length of service. This can be taken as either ordinary maternity leave (the first 26 weeks) or additional maternity leave (the remaining 26 weeks).
- Maternity pay: Eligible pregnant employees are entitled to statutory maternity pay (SMP) for up to 39 weeks. This is paid at a rate of 90% of their average weekly earnings for the first six weeks, followed by £172.48 per week (or 90% of their average weekly earnings, whichever is lower) for the remaining 33 weeks.
- Health and safety: Employers must carry out a risk assessment to ensure that the pregnant employee is not exposed to any risks that could harm her or the baby. If there are risks

present, the employer must take steps to eliminate or reduce them.
- Protection against discrimination: Pregnant employees are protected against discrimination and harassment on the grounds of pregnancy or maternity. This includes protection against dismissal, less favourable treatment, and unfavourable changes to their terms and conditions of employment.

These regulations apply to all pregnant employees, regardless of their length of service or the size of their employer's business.

In the UK to be entitled to Statutory Maternity Pay (SMP), a pregnant employee must meet certain criteria, including:

- They must be an employee, not a worker or self-employed.
- They must have given their employer the correct notice of their pregnancy and intention to take maternity leave. The notice

must be in writing and include the expected date of childbirth and the date on which they intend to start their maternity leave.
- They must have been continuously employed by their employer for at least 26 weeks up to and including the 15th week before the expected week of childbirth (known as the qualifying week).
- They must earn at least £123 per week on average. This is the current rate as of April 2023 and does change. This is known as the Lower Earnings Level (LEL).
- If a pregnant employee meets these criteria, they will be entitled to receive SMP for up to 39 weeks. The first six weeks are paid at 90% of their average weekly earnings, followed by the rate of Statutory Maternity Pay (or 90% of their average weekly earnings, whichever is lower) for the remaining 33 weeks. If the

employee is not eligible for SMP, they may still be entitled to Maternity Allowance from the government.

## What happens with benefits during maternity leave?

During maternity leave, an employee is still classed as employed and therefore all their contractual rights and benefits still apply, except for those linked to remuneration. 'Remuneration' is money paid for work or a service, normally referred to as wages. Most employment contracts will refer to this term, stipulating the terms of conditions of employment in relation to wages under the heading 'Remuneration'.

Employees on maternity leave are still entitled to benefits not linked to remuneration such as holiday allowance, EAP, Cash Plans, private health/medical insurance, childcare vouchers, and pension contributions, for the entire time they are on maternity leave.

To identify whether an employee is entitled to continue receiving their bonus as a benefit during their maternity leave is dependent on the type of bonus, contractual or discretionary.

Bonus payments that form part of salary or normal earnings are usually regarded as remuneration and therefore an employee would not be entitled to it during their maternity leave.

If employees are paid an annual bonus, the employee on maternity leave should be paid the bonus pro-rate to cover the period in which the employee was at work.

If any employer pays an employee a discretionary bonus each month for taking on an extra role or responsibility, which is outside of their contractual agreement, the employee could argue that this could be deemed as a benefit they receive and therefore should continue to receive it during their maternity leave. This is why we would encourage employers to document this additional payment as part of Remuneration in the employment contract.

It's always advisable to ensure any form of benefit or remuneration an employee receives is written into their Terms and Conditions of Employment to avoid confusion.

## Sharing Maternity Leave

Since 2015, eligible parents can share parental leave and pay with their partner under the Shared Parental Leave (SPL) scheme. Here's how it works:

1. Eligibility: To be eligible for SPL, the mother or adopter must be eligible for maternity/adoption leave, and the partner must meet the eligibility criteria for paternity leave and pay or be eligible for adoption leave and pay.
2. Notice: The mother or adopter must give notice to their employer to end their maternity/adoption leave and to share the remaining leave with their partner. The notice must be given at

least 8 weeks before the start of the first period of SPL.
3. Agreement: The mother's employer and the partner's employer must agree to the SPL arrangement, including the start and end dates and the pattern of leave.
4. Entitlement: The parents can share up to 50 weeks of leave and up to 37 weeks of pay between them. They can take the leave in a continuous block or in separate blocks and can take it at the same time or separately.
5. Pay: The pay for SPL is at the statutory rate, which is currently £172.48 per week or 90% of average weekly earnings, whichever is lower. Parents can take up to 3 blocks of SPL with periods of work in between and can claim pay during each block of leave.

Shared Parental Leave (SPL) isn't a popular choice for working parents in the UK. According to a survey conducted by the Department for Business, Energy, and

Industrial Strategy in 2018, only 9% of eligible parents had taken up the opportunity to share their leave.

There are several factors that may contribute to the low uptake of SPL, including:

- Awareness: Many parents may not be aware of the SPL scheme or may not fully understand how it works.
- Eligibility: Not all parents are eligible for SPL, as both parents must meet certain criteria, such as having worked for their employer for a minimum period of time.
- Financial considerations: SPL is paid at the statutory rate, which is currently £151.97 per week or 90% of average weekly earnings, whichever is lower. Some families may not be able to afford to take SPL, particularly if one parent earns significantly more than the other.
- Workplace culture: Some parents may feel that taking SPL could harm their

career prospects or lead to discrimination in the workplace.

Despite the low uptake of SPL, it remains an important policy tool for promoting gender equality and supporting parents in balancing work and caring responsibilities. The government has announced plans to review the scheme and explore ways to increase its uptake, including through greater promotion and awareness-raising.

Where we see Early Years and Childcare employers having requests for Shared Parental Leave it is where a mother to be has a better paid role than her partner and they both work in the same setting.

## Supporting your employees with their IVF journey

It is important to note that while there may not be a statutory right to time off specifically for IVF treatment, employers are encouraged to be understanding and considerate of their employees' needs. Engaging in open and honest communication with the employer about the reasons for needing time off and exploring possible solutions can often lead to mutually beneficial arrangements.

In recent years more and more employees have been grateful that their employers have a IVF Policy, clearly setting out what they can expect if they start fertility treatment during their employment.

IVF itself is a common and yet much understood workplace issue and one that needs Line Manager's to be both supportive yet consistent with their policy.

So, what can you do to help support those going through IVF Treatment? Infertility affects around 3.5 million people in the UK according to the NHS. That's around 1 in 7 couples. Many who undergo IVF treatment are women over 35 years of age and increasing numbers self-fund. Infertility is a medical problem and employers should ensure their approach to supporting employees with IVF is no different to how they would support their employee with any other medical issue.

Let's not forget partners. Those who love someone who is undergoing the physical IVF treatment is also in need of our support as their employer. It's as important that partners can have open and honest conversations with their Line Managers about their concerns. Otherwise, it can lead to time being lost through stress.

We feel the key to creating a supportive and consistent environment is communication. The employer needs to encourage open conversation between the parties. What one woman undergoing IVF wants may be very different from another woman. For example, some women are very private and want to talk about support but additionally insist that their decision to seek fertility treatment is confidential. Others want to tell everyone in order to feel their support and want you to be open and honest with others regarding their situation. Both approaches can cause problems for the employer.

Additionally, we would encourage the employer who operates a Day Nursery, Pre-school, or Out of School Club to consider how their workplace may impact a woman contemplating, undergoing or recovering from IVF treatment. No one size fits all and the adoption of a IVF policy is a start that is followed by open and honest communication.

Common questions that women undertaking IVF may have:

- Can I have time off for the treatments? The law doesn't give time off for IVF treatment until after the embryo has been implanted.
- Can I reduce my workload whilst I am having treatment? There's nothing to stop employers and employees coming to a temporary flexible working arrangement and this is to be encouraged.
- Can I have a room to take my injections/pessaries during the working day? We can all agree the toilet isn't appropriate.

- Can I have somewhere quiet to go when it's all too much? IVF has a greater than 50% failure rate so women who return to work following a failed IVF treatment may find working with babies and toddlers particularly difficult. Phrases like you can try again and there's always next time can be particularly unhelpful. An EAP might be a great place to sign post the employee to.

## Holiday & Leave

Employees are entitled to a statutory holiday entitlement, which refers to the minimum amount of paid leave they are entitled to receive. Employers are free to give more leave than the statutory entitlement, many in Early Years and Childcare choose to reward long term The statutory holiday entitlement in the UK is governed by the Working Time Regulations 1998. Here are the key points:

Annual Leave Entitlement: Full-time employees are entitled to a minimum of 5.6 weeks (or 28 days) of paid annual leave per year. Part-time employees are also entitled to annual leave, calculated on a pro-rata basis according to their working hours.

For example, if you work 4 days a week which is compressed working and common in Early Years and Childcare your pro rata entitlement will be 4 x 5.6 weeks which is 22.4 days.

In the UK, there are typically eight bank holidays, such as Christmas Day, New Year's Day, and Easter Monday. However, in Scotland there is a nine. However, bank holidays do not have to be given as paid leave unless stated in the employment contract.

The statutory holiday entitlement can't be carried over to the next year if the employee hasn't been able to use all their annual leave. There are exceptions to this rule when an employee has been long term sick or where they have been on maternity or adoption leave.

Employers are expected to encourage employees to take the leave they are due and can fix holidays if this is allowed in the contract of employment.

In July 2022 it was confirmed by the Supreme Court in the case of Brazel vs Harpur Trust that term time only employees could not have less than 5.6 weeks holiday entitlement.

## Contracts of employment

There are three types of contracts used in Early Years and Childcare where holiday calculations are an issue. These are:

- Casual or Zero Hours contracts
- Term time only contracts
- Variable hours contracts

Before July 2022 we used 12.07% of hours worked to calculate annual leave for Casual and Variable hours contracts. 12.07% is derived from 5.6 weeks/46.4 weeks =0.120689. Multiplied by 100 = 12.07%. The Supreme Court confirmed what had already been decided by the Court of Appeal that this calculated placed Mrs Brazel at a disadvantage and that as a zero hour term time only worker she should have 5.6 weeks of leave calculated by finding an average weeks pay from the 12 weeks of work before the leave was taken. This has since been replaced by a 52-week reference period.

So, what does this mean for employers in Early Years and Childcare? Sadly, it means lots of calculations. For many a spreadsheet will need to be maintained for the casual and variable hours employees. For calculating the entitlement of people who join or leave during the holiday year we would recommend you use the Government's online calculator found here:

https://www.gov.uk/calculate-your-holiday-entitlement

We are expecting changes to how holiday entitlement is calculated when the Working Time Regulations are eventually amended.

# Time off for Family Emergencies

All employees have the right to take time off work to deal with unexpected or sudden family emergencies. This is also known as Time off for Dependants, and it is a legal entitlement under the Employment Rights Act 1996. Here are the key rules:

- Definition of a dependant: A dependant can be a spouse, partner, child, parent, or someone else who depends on the employee for care, such as an elderly relative or a disabled family member.
- Reasonable amount of time off: The amount of time off allowed is considered reasonable in the circumstances and can vary depending on the situation. It is typically limited to one or two days, but in some cases, more time may be required.
- Notification: Employees should notify their employer of their need to take time off as soon as possible and

provide details of the emergency and how long they expect to be away from work.
- Paid or unpaid: There is no statutory right to be paid for time off for dependants, but some employers may offer paid time off as part of their contractual terms or policy.
- Disciplinary action: Employers are not allowed to take disciplinary action against an employee for taking time off for dependants, as long as the time off is reasonable in the circumstances.

It's important to note that time off for dependants is only intended for unexpected or sudden emergencies, such as a family member falling ill, or a child's school being closed unexpectedly. It cannot be used as a substitute for regular childcare arrangements or for planned absences, such as attending a family wedding or holiday.

# Time off for personal appointments

What do you do if an employee suddenly informs in the middle of their shift, without notice, that they need to go out to a doctor's appointment in an hours' time? Or any other personal appointment?

What about a midwife appointment? It's not a personal appointment but surely if it's a pregnant employee, they have the right to do so. Absolutely not. All requests have to be reasonable.

Let's take regular appointments first. It's not unreasonable to say as an employer, that personal appointments need to be taken at the beginning or end of the working day. Perhaps they work a reduced working week and can take appointments on their non-working day.

Whilst time off for appointments would be covered in the employee handbook, we are unreasonable people. We know that it's not always possible to get (for example) a doctor's appointment at a time to suit.

So what can you do in this situation? You can refuse it. If you've not been given any notice or advance warning, and it proves a logistical nightmare, you can refuse it. You have to consider the impact this could have on your remaining employees and maintaining quality standards. However, if you can accommodate be wary that this will then become the expectation in the future. Be clear that you will grant it 'on this occasion' should you choose to do so. Remind them of the policies regarding personal appointments, and you can't guarantee a request at this short notice can be granted again.

If an employee is unwell but can attend work, encourage dialogue as it may be a case that the employee does need to seek a medical appointment, and you can mutually agree on this and how to make it workable for both parties.

If you have a pregnant employee who suddenly declares they have an antenatal appointment in an hour, then that's not ok. Section 55 of the Employment Rights Act 1996 covers the employees right to time off for antenatal appointments. Antenatal appointments are scheduled, and you are entitled to ask for a list of scheduled appointments in advance. If it's an emergency and the woman and child's health is at risk, then that's a different matter.

As an employer, you have a duty to the health and welfare of your employees, and in this case, their unborn child. You are within your rights to add to your maternity policy that the appointment card must be shown. A pregnant employee is entitled to reasonable time off with pay for antenatal appointments. As always, the issue is the definition of the word reasonableness.

We've heard of cases whereby an employee suddenly needs to go to their solicitor as they're going through a messy divorce. Again, you want to help where you can, but it can't always be accommodated. It's ok to say no.

Regardless of the need to attend a personal appointment, you can request proof of this by way of an appointment letter/ confirmation, or an appointment card. Reasonableness remember, is a 2-way street!

# What about time off to attend appointments with a partner?

Employees have certain rights when it comes to attending antenatal appointments with their partner. These rights are outlined in the Employment Rights Act 1996 and the Maternity and Parental Leave Regulations 1999. Here's an explanation of an employee's right to unpaid time off for antenatal appointments:

To be eligible for this right, the employee must be the partner of a pregnant woman and have a qualifying relationship with her, such as being the biological father, spouse, or civil partner.

An employee has the right to take a reasonable amount of time off work to accompany their pregnant partner to antenatal appointments. This includes medical examinations, classes, or any other necessary appointments related to the pregnancy.

There is no fixed duration for the time off, but it should be a reasonable amount of time to attend the appointment and travel to and from the appointment location. Generally, a few hours should be sufficient for most appointments, but it may vary depending on the circumstances.

The employee is required to provide reasonable notice to their employer before taking time off for antenatal appointments. This notice should include the date and time of the appointment and the length of time the employee expects to be away from work. Additionally, the employer may ask for evidence of the appointment, such as an appointment card or letter.

The right to attend antenatal appointments is unpaid leave. However, some employers may have policies in place that provide paid time off for such appointments, so it's essential to check the company's policies or employment contract.

Employees are protected from being subjected to any unfair treatment or dismissal due to taking time off for antenatal appointments. It is unlawful for employers to treat employees detrimentally or dismiss them because of their exercise of this right.

It's important to note that these rights apply specifically to the employee attending the appointments with their partner.

## Adoption Leave

Adoption leave in the UK is designed to provide support and time off for employees who are adopting a child. The entitlements and rights regarding adoption leave are outlined in the Adoption and Children Act 2002 and the Employment Rights Act 1996. Here's an explanation of adoption leave in the UK:

- Eligibility: To be eligible for adoption leave, an employee must be newly matched with a child for adoption through an approved adoption agency. They should be an employee (not self-

employed) and have completed a minimum period of continuous employment, which is usually 26 weeks by the time they are matched with a child.
- Notification and evidence: The employee must inform their employer in writing about their intention to take adoption leave, including the expected date of placement and the date they plan to start their leave. They should provide this notice at least 28 days before the intended start of their leave. Additionally, the employer may require evidence of the adoption, such as an official notification from the adoption agency.
- Ordinary Adoption Leave (OAL): Employees are entitled to 26 weeks of Ordinary Adoption Leave, regardless of their length of service. During this period, the employee retains their usual employment rights, such as the right to receive their contractual benefits, except for remuneration.

- Additional Adoption Leave (AAL): After completing 26 weeks of adoption leave, employees may be entitled to take a further 26 weeks of Additional Adoption Leave. During this period, the employee's employment rights continue to be protected, although some contractual benefits may differ or be limited.
- Statutory Adoption Pay (SAP): Statutory Adoption Pay is a financial benefit that eligible employees can receive during their adoption leave. It changes every April and is currently £172.48 per week. For the first six weeks of adoption leave, employees are entitled to 90% of their average weekly earnings (pre-tax), and for the remaining weeks, they receive the lower of either the statutory flat rate or 90% of their average weekly earnings (whichever is lower).
- Return to work: At the end of the adoption leave period, the employee has the right to return to their

previous job, or if that is not reasonably practicable, a suitable alternative job with the same terms and conditions. The employer should not subject the employee to any unfair treatment or dismissal due to taking adoption leave.

## Does an employee have any rights when they become foster parents?

Currently, the UK's foster carers employment laws determine that only in a "foster to adopt" situation is a statutory right for employers to pay time-off to employees who foster a child.

Should your staff member be both a local authority foster parent and a prospective adopter, the employee could find themselves in a "foster to adopt" situation. If that is the case, they will be protected by foster care employment law and entitled to adoption leave and pay.

So, are foster parents' employment rights the same as regular employment rights? Parental Leave does not cover leave for foster parents. Only if the child is adopted parental leave for foster parents would be set at 18 weeks of and can be taken during the five years following the date of the adoption or until the child's 18th birthday.

Flexible working, however, is an appropriate way to manage any staff members who are foster carers. Employment rights say that employees with at least 26 weeks of continuous service have the right to request flexible working. Eligible employees can use this right to suggest working hours that give their dependants a comfortable home life. You are not legally bound to agree to flexible working requests automatically. However, you are required to reasonably handle all requests for parental leave for foster parents through flexible working hours. You can only refuse if the request does not reconcile with a specific list of legitimate business reasons.

Under the Employment Rights Act 1996, all employees (regardless of the length of service) can take a 'reasonable' amount of unpaid time off work without notice to deal with unexpected emergencies affecting their dependents. Children within a foster care situation would count as dependent as they rely on the employee.

## Flexible Working

Where employee who works at setting wishes to make a flexible working request to reduce their hours of work. There are steps they would need to follow:

1. Check eligibility: The employee must have worked for their employer for at least 26 weeks to be eligible to make a flexible working request.

2. Put the request in writing: The employee must make a written request to their employer, explaining the change they are seeking (in this

case, a reduction in hours) and when they would like the change to take effect.

3. Explain the reason for the request: The employee should explain why they are making the request, such as to care for a child or to manage a health condition. In the future we expect this requirement to be dropped but I do think it is always a good idea for the employee to explain why to their employer. Employers are human!

4. Consider alternative arrangements: The employee should also suggest any alternative arrangements that could help meet the needs of the business while also accommodating their request, such as changing their work hours or job sharing. In the future employers who need to reject flexible working requests will be expected to consider alternatives or compromises that they could accommodate and to

put these forward for the employee to consider.

5. Follow the employer's process: The employer must consider the request and respond within three months. They may want to hold a meeting with the employee to discuss the request in more detail.

6. Appeal process: If the employer refuses the request, the employee can appeal the decision. They should follow the employer's appeals process, which should be set out in their policy.

While employers must consider flexible working requests, they are not obliged to grant them if there are legitimate business reasons for refusing them. Currently there are 8 reasons in the regulations that mean an employer can reject a flexible working request. We do not expect these reasons to change when the regulations are next updated.

1. Burden of additional costs: The requested changes would result in additional costs that would have a detrimental effect on the business.
2. Detrimental effect on ability to meet customer demand: The requested changes would have a detrimental effect on the employer's ability to meet customer demand.
3. Inability to reorganize work among existing staff: The requested changes would not be possible without reorganizing the work among existing staff, and the employer considers this impractical.
4. Inability to recruit additional staff: The requested changes would not be possible without recruiting additional staff, and the employer considers this impractical.
5. Detrimental impact on quality: The requested changes would have a detrimental effect on the quality of the work done by the employee or by other employees.

6. Detrimental impact on performance: The requested changes would have a detrimental effect on the performance of the employee or of the employer's business.
7. Insufficient work during the periods the employee proposes to work: The employee's proposed working arrangements would result in the employee not having enough work during the periods they propose to work.
8. Planned structural changes: The employer has planned structural changes to the business that would make the employees proposed working.

Whilst the employer can reject a request for one or more of the above reasons, they must be able to demonstrate that the reason is genuine and not just a cover for discrimination or other unfair treatment. Employers should consider each request on a case-by-case basis and provide a clear and specific reason for any decision to reject a request.

# Menopause

ACAS has published useful guidance on how to manage menopause at work and its fair to say there has never been such recognition about the impact of the menopause for working women. The CIPD says that 59% of women who experience menopausal symptoms said that it impacted them negatively at work.

There are many ways that a woman may experience menopausal symptoms:

- Firstly, the environment, hot sweats can be both embarrassing and debilitating. Imagine being asked to where polyester uniform and trousers when you are experiencing fluctuating temperatures that you can't control.
- Performance: women report problems with concentration, brain fog, headaches and anxiety all of which impact performance.
- Disclosure; we all love talking about heavy periods, don't we? No, being

embarrassed and being anxious about how the Line Manager will react are all described as reasons why disclosure makes women uncomfortable.

Why does it matter how manager's manage employees experiencing menopause?

It isn't just best practice to manage menopause effectively. The Equality Act 2010 can create liability on employers. Symptoms can be severe and last 12 months, say no more!

The employer is therefore under a duty to make reasonable adjustments for the employees impacted by the menopause. Equally they must ensure that they do not directly or indirectly discriminate.

In Davies v Scottish Courts and Tribunal Service, Mrs Davies won her tribunal as she was suffering with the menopause. Her condition caused her to be forgetful and confused and this behaviour led to her dismissal from her job. Her employer failed to take into consideration that her condition was a disability.

Apart from losing tribunals for unfair dismissal. Employers could also find themselves on the wrong side of the Equality Act 2010 if an employee was to allege harassment. Unwanted comments could be made about people going through the menopause. We all know how quickly jokes can go south these days.

Your uniform policy could be indirectly discriminatory if they disadvantage women who have symptoms of the menopause. Therefore, you need to create an environment where these women can come to you and discuss what adjustments they need, and you can then reflect whether you can be flexible with your uniform policy.

Managers should be trained in the policy and can benefit from taking part in a course regardless of their stage in life or gender.

If employees know that managers are trained and competent, they are more likely to approach their manager.

In summary if workplaces are more understanding of the effects that the menopause may have on women, and are prepared to adjust assist women, more women will feel comfortable discussing it. The more it's talked about, the less it is a taboo and the less likely you are to face a tribunal.

## Absence

We often here anecdotally that employees can take 28 weeks of statutory sick pay and there's nothing the employer can do about it. Under employment law that statement is not correct.

An employee who meets the eligibility criteria (has commenced employment, would earn over the lower earnings threshold) can receive up to 28 weeks of Statutory Sick Pay (SSP) from an employer in any 12-month period. This means that the maximum amount of SSP that an employer will pay will be in the region of 28 weeks before the employee will be given a SSP1 form to take to the Job Centre Plus.

We encourage employers to manage absenteeism in their Day Nurseries, Pre-schools or Out of School Clubs. If an employee's absence is unmanaged, they are more likely to struggle to return to work after a long-term absence, or more likely to take regular time off work in the terms of short-term sickness absence.

The employment relationship is hinged upon the idea that the employee will attend work regularly, not just when they don't have a better offer!

To understand the relationship between employment law and sickness absence we need to explain certain aspects. These include:

1. Self-certification. Employers should require employees to self-certify for the first 7 calendar days of absence. These notes should be completed and signed by the employee and filed securely in their personnel record.
2. Statements of Fitness for Work also known as Fit Notes. These should be required of all employees whose

absence has lasted more than 7 calendar days. The Statement can since July 2022 be provided by a medical professional such as a pharmacists, occupational health, or nurse in addition to a GP. In practice most of the Statements of Fitness for Work are provided by GPs though often this is handled over a telephone conversation.

3. Sickness Absence Reporting – employers are entitled to determine their own sickness absence reporting procedures. These will often still require the employee to telephone their line manager before a certain time on the first day of absence. Despite a propensity for employees to prefer to text or send a social media message there is nothing to stop an employer insisting that they are contacted in person in the first instance.

4. Waiting Days- When it comes to Statutory Sick Pay (SSP) the first 3

days are known as waiting days. These first 3 days do not attract SSP. If the employee remains unfit for work on day 4, the employee commences receiving SSP from day 4 onwards. If the employee has a linked absence (within 56 days) they do not serve two lots of waiting days. However, this doesn't mean that they can have odd days off that attract SSP. The new, linked absence still has to last longer than 4 days to count.

5. Company Sick Pay. There is nothing in law that compels an employer to offer Company or organisational sick pay. Small businesses often can't afford to offer such schemes and if they do, they are often limited in terms of their scope. If Company Sick Pay is part of the terms and conditions, it can be expected that the employer is able to wait for the company sick pay to be exhausted before they seek to terminate on the grounds of capability. However, this is not a hard and fast

rule. Some employers have fairly terminated an employee who is long term sick and still has unpaid Company Sick Pay.
6. Employee Assistance Programmes. These are a great way to support employees to who may otherwise be off sick. An Employee Assistance Programme can be purchased as a benefit for employees through a number of providers in the UK. Again, no employer is compelled to offer EAP, but it does demonstrate a commitment to staff wellbeing.

# Handling a Short-Term Absence issue

In your Early Years and Childcare setting if you have an employee who is absent regularly your first step should be to track and plot the absences to see if there is a pattern. Once someone's absence is an issue, then the first step is to meet with the employee informally to make them aware that you are concerned regarding their attendance. It's perfectly reasonable to speak to an employee with whom you have concerns regarding their attendance, if you do not speak to them, you do not give yourself or them the opportunity to explore the reason for the absence and what if anything you can do to help them. I remember once speaking to an employee about their lateness only to find that they struggled to get a bus to work, they needed assistance to make sure they got on the right bus. We would never have realised this unless we sat down and spoke.

If an informal conversation doesn't address the issue, then the next step might be a more formal conversation under the disciplinary procedure. Calling someone into a disciplinary hearing regarding their attendance would involve attaching evidence of their absences to the letter.

# What happens when someone wants to leave?

Sadly, not all hires will stay. In fact, some people don't say very long at all. I once had someone ask for the toilet during their initial Health and Safety induction on their first morning. He headed for the exit, and we never saw him again. I've also heard of settings where the new hire never starts. Firstly, they have a car accident, then the dog dies and by week three the employer has given up all hope of the new starter commencing employment. The net effect the job offer is withdrawn.

So, what happens from an employment law perspective if your employee wants to resign from your employment. Well firstly no employee must stay. You can't drag an employee kicking and screaming down the road to come to work if they don't want to!

The contract of employment will inform the parties of the required minimum notice period if they wish to terminate the contract. I say minimum as there is nothing in employment law to stop an employee giving you much longer notice. We do see this in practice in Early Years and Childcare. It can be a bit awkward. Imagine the scene, you are advised by an employee that they are resigning with a year's notice. They then spend the next year not wanting to be there, but the employer cannot do anything unless they want to take the risk to dismiss the employee.

In a typical situation the resigning employee will consult their contract of employment and then either give you their notice period or will give you what they feel is the notice they want to give. In employment law we can address a failure to give contractual notice as a breach of contract, but there can be few benefits of this.

We recommend that in the contract of employment the employer states that the employer may choose to withhold the additional cost of cover if they do not give their contractual notice from their final pay.

The employee should provide their employer with their resignation in writing. This can now involve a text, WhatsApp message, email or piece of paper left on the Manager's desk. In the contract of employment, it should advise employees that they should not discuss their resignation with their colleagues, parents, or the children before they have had their resignation acknowledged by their employer.

In acknowledging the resignation, we should formally write to the employee setting out their date of termination and what you want them to do, i.e., return an any Company owned equipment such as uniform and by when.

In terms of deductions the contract of employment will often set out that the employer will reserve the right in addition to the deduction for the cost of cover, to deduct any overpayment of holiday, to deduct the cost of uniform if not returned, to deduct the cost of keys, company equipment etc on termination of employment.

Where the employee struggles to calculate the holiday entitlement that has been accrued during the holiday year, we recommend they use the Government's online calculator. This works if the holiday entitlement in the full holiday year is the statutory minimum of 5.6 weeks. By putting in the date of termination, and the date the holiday year began, the employer will receive the entitlement which they can then compare with what holiday has been already taken.

## Do I have to give sick pay to my employee who has had elective or cosmetic surgery?

Let's initially discuss what elective and cosmetic surgery includes. First of which is elective, this is defined as any surgery that is scheduled in advance, for example where there is no emergency and can include surgery that does improve someone's health and appearance for example where someone is suffering depression due to a birth mark or where they have a gastric band fitted for weight loss etc.

Remember to think broadly about health and think psychological health as well as physical health.

By contrast, cosmetic surgery is often used to describe the surgery which is again planned but doesn't need to be undertaken on any health grounds, i.e., nose jobs, tummy tucks, boob jobs. There are also have cosmetic procedures such as Botox, lip fillers etc that aren't classed as surgery but can result in an employee being absent from work.

What happens when an employee tells you they are planning surgery?

Discovering that your employee will be absent from work as they plan to have elective surgery means that you should discuss with the employee what they will be paid for their absence.

They could request holiday or unpaid leave for the procedure. Whether you can authorise this will depend on the impact on your Day Nursery, Pre-school or Club. Holiday requests can be refused if you already have staff off, as can requests for unpaid time off.

So, what should your employee do if they wish to have elective or cosmetic surgery that will impact their employment?

In an ideal world the employee will meet with their Line Manager to discuss their plans. Don't be surprised if this doesn't happen. In society we can be judgemental towards others who seek to improve their appearance (in their view) and they may feel uncomfortable sharing their plans with their employer for fear of judgement. In strict terms the employee is under no obligation to advise you as to what they intend to do with their annual leave.

Where the employee takes annual leave that is authorised the expectation is that they will return on the date that they said they would, if they are unfit to resume work, we would advise you treat as any employee who is unable to return from annual leave due to sickness absence.

Whilst the procedure may have been planned, frequently the recovery will be unplanned and in most cases the recovery period means that the employee is genuinely unfit to resume work.

Again, you'd like to think that the employee will discuss this with you and whether they would be fit if their role was adjusted or modified during their recovery. The employer doesn't have to accommodate a request for adjusted or modified duties if it doesn't work for the business.

In terms of whether the recovery period is paid, or unpaid sickness absence will depend on your Absence policy.

If you pay SSP you will be familiar that the first 3 days of the absence are waiting days and only if they are off for 4 or more days does the employee start to accrue SSP from day 4. The employee can self-certify their absence for 7 calendar days so will not need a Statement of Fitness for Work till day 8. If the employee has had surgery overseas, they may struggle to obtain an overseas medical certificate for their continued absence.

If they are entitled to CSP they will be due to be paid for their sick leave unless you have a clause in the contract which gives you the right to withhold sick pay. Be careful if you have this, and we certainly wouldn't recommend one. The reason why someone might be seeking elective surgery may be covered under the Equality Act 2010. Severe disfigurement is one that comes to mind.

Remember, health information is deemed as sensitive employee data under Data Protection Regulations.

Don't share the nature of the employee's absence with their colleagues. They have the right to have their health matters treated with strict confidentiality.

# Baby Sitting

From time to time the question arises as to whether it would be an issue if staff are involved in babysitting for the children who attend the nursery. In the past I have seen notices in Nurseries advertising the staff who can babysit your child, though these signs of endorsement seem to be a thing of the past.

There is no employment right for an employee to baby sit the children of your customers outside of work.

From a HR perspective I think there are several things to consider before you decide on your approach to babysitting, these may include:

- How does staff babysitting the children possibly impact on the staff member's ability to be objective and safeguard that child. Babysitting is often seen as a safeguarding issue. No one wants to see 'lines blurred'.
- If the only reason the parent knows of the babysitter, is you; would they believe you are responsible for the transaction? If the staff member lets them down, will you be asked to get involved?

- What about this question of liability? Can an employer really wash their hands of any liability when as we've said before, you introduced the staff member to the parent, they work with the child during the day, you've said they are trained and qualified. Would your disclaimer be effective or ineffective, do you know?
- What happens if the unthinkable happens? You will have a staff member who can't function, a parent who will be looking for someone to blame, a child no longer at your setting, and the press will go to town that he/she was babysitting for the child at the time.
- What about income? Staff who babysit should be registered self-employed, pay tax on their second income, and have their own professional liability and public liability insurance.
- What would your insurer say about the arrangement?
- What about confidentiality, could it be breached more easily with this

arrangement? We've seen parents 'tap the babysitter up for information' about another family because the conversation was in their living room, and they felt they could.
- What if the parents alleged that your staff member had abused their child? What would that mean?
- Can you add something to your contract with the parents that covers babysitting, would you enforce the clause if you needed to?
- What if the staff member saw something and they reported it to the relevant authorities, what would that mean?
- What about when the parent's sexually harass the staff. We have had several situations over the years where parents have made what we will call for the purpose of this book 'advances. What happens when this in the dad's car when's he's driving the babysitter home? You would never forgive yourselves. You don't DBS the parents!

- What about the ages of the children, your staff member may be experienced with older children and look after a baby.
- What if they use the paediatric first aid training you paid for and got it wrong, would you be liable?

In conclusion, we advise you take advise from your LA, safeguarding professionals and your peers and decide upon your own approach. Sadly, I don't think it is as easy as saying it happens outside of work, so it's none of our business. It can easily become your business.

# Training

Training in Early Years and Childcare often falls into two distinct categories. Training that is mandatory and training that is developmental.

Training that is mandatory is either training that has been specified as forming part of the contract of employment for example that all staff will undertake Paediatric First Aid or training that is required for the role for example safeguarding training.

The cost of mandatory training cannot be deducted from wages if the deduction takes the employee below the National Minimum Wage. However, if you set that if an employee has to pay for a mandatory course if they fail to attend and the reason for their non-attendance is not acceptable to the employer in their Written Statement of Terms and Conditions then you can deduct as it is now a conduct issue much in the same way as it is permissible to deduct unreturned Company uniform.

Training that an employee undertakes for their own development may be deducted from wages under certain circumstances.

For example, if the employee asks the employer to allow them to undertake a forest school qualification and the employee then withdraws from the course. The employer would have recourse only if the parties entered into a training clawback agreement before the commencement of the forest school qualification. Don't forget these clawbacks should be securely stored. On far to many occasions I have had an employer complain to me that they can't find their copy of the signed training clawback agreement. Without they can't deduct anything.

Training and training plans form an important part of the employment relationship.

We always describe roles in Early Years and Childcare to be skilled roles with sadly low pay. There is a great expectation that early year's educators will be well qualified to do their role and in Childcare we have PARS qualifications that are popular way of being qualified in play work.

There is no requirement in employment law for smaller businesses to give employees time off for training. This requirement does exist for larger employers. Smaller employers are expected to cover the training cost and the time an employer is training. For example, if you purchase a login for your Early Years Practitioner and they can then access the online learning platform to undertake a course, you are responsible for the cost of the login plus the cost of any time they spend training. This is because training time equals working time and they must receive at least the National Minimum Wage when undertaking training. Less than this and they could claim that you are in breach of the National Minimum Wage.

## Whistleblowing

Whistleblowing is the act of reporting wrongdoing or concerns about certain practices or behaviours that might cause harm to individuals or an organisation.

In the context of Early Years and Childcare, whistleblowing is essential to ensure the safety and well-being of children. By adopting a whistleblowing policy, Early Years and Childcare organisations can provide a clear framework for employees to report concerns and ensure that they are investigated and addressed appropriately.

One of the main benefits of having a whistleblowing policy in place is that it can help to prevent and address allegations of failures to safeguard children in Early Years and Childcare settings. A whistleblowing policy encourages employees to report any concerns they may have ensured that any such issues are addressed promptly and appropriately.

It's sadly the case that it can be new starters or students that identify something isn't right and raise the alarm. The serious case review into Little Stars in Birmingham found that it was students who raised the alarm by whistleblowing to their college tutors who in turn raised the alarm with the LADO for Birmingham.

Adopting a whistleblowing policy is a requirement for Early Years and Childcare employers. Under the Public Interest Disclosure Act (PIDA) 199, employees are provided with legal protection where they report wrongdoing in the workplace.

## Compassionate Leave

Whilst employees are granted several rights and benefits to ensure their well-being and work-life balance there is no blanket right to compassionate leave.

Compassionate leave, also sometimes referred to as bereavement leave or compassionate time off, is a type of leave granted to employees to provide them with time and flexibility to deal with a family or personal emergency. This leave allows employees to attend to critical situations that arise due to the illness, injury, or death of a close family member or dependant. Employees should provide these documents promptly to facilitate the leave process.

Employees have the right to parental bereavement leave in the UK. Parental Bereavement Leave (PBL) is a statutory entitlement in the United Kingdom that allows eligible employees to take time off work following the death of a child. It is designed to provide support and flexibility to parents who experience the devastating loss of a child.

Paid bereavement leave applies to all employed parents who suffer the loss of a child under the age of 18, including adoptive parents, foster parents, and legal guardians. Both mothers and fathers have the right to take this leave.

Employees must inform their employer about their intention to take parental bereavement leave, specifying the start date, as soon as reasonably practicable. This notice should be given within a reasonable timeframe, usually within one week of the child's death.

Eligible employees are entitled to a minimum of two weeks of Parental Bereavement Leave. This period is known as "Statutory Parental Bereavement Leave" (SPBL). Employees may take the leave as a continuous block or as separate periods, depending on their needs and agreement with their employer.

Statutory Parental Bereavement Pay (SPBP) is also available for eligible employees who meet specific criteria. SPBP is paid at the statutory rate, which is reviewed and updated annually. To qualify for SPBP, employees must have completed a certain period of continuous service with their employer.

Employees who take SPBL are required to inform their employer about their intention to return to work. This notice should be given at least one week before the intended return date, unless otherwise agreed with the employer.

Employees have legal protection against unfair treatment or dismissal due to their request for Parental Bereavement Leave. Employers must not discriminate against employees who exercise their rights under this entitlement.

Parental Bereavement Leave can be taken within 56 weeks following the child's death. This provides parents with flexibility to take time off at a time that suits their emotional needs, such as around anniversaries or other significant dates.

It is important to note that the specific details and policies regarding Parental Bereavement Leave may vary between employers. Therefore, employees are advised to consult their employment contracts or company policies for accurate information regarding their entitlement to leave and pay during such difficult times.

The introduction of Parental Bereavement Leave in the UK reflects the recognition of the profound impact the loss of a child has on parents and aims to provide them with essential time and support to grieve and recover. Employers may request appropriate documentation, such as a death certificate and it would be our advice to be sensitive in this situation. Just because the law gives you the right to ask for evidence of the loss of a child in the form of a death certificate doesn't mean you should.

Compassionate leave will depend on the employer's policies and procedures and should be consulted if it is to be paid compassionate leave.

Whilst there may be no right to compassionate leave (except in the circumstances mentioned above) there are other rights that may come into play when there has been a bereavement. These include:

Right to Reasonable Time Off: Employees have the right to take a reasonable amount of unpaid leave to deal with a personal emergency or family crisis. The specific time off may vary depending on the situation and the needs of the individual.

## Supporting a bereaved employee with their religious observance

When someone dies, relatives will want to ensure that they follow the family's customs and traditions when it comes to the death.

For many people their family customs and traditions involve religious observance, and as an employer we need to be informed as to what our employee's might request under religious observance when they are bereaved.

When approached by a bereaved employee asking for time off following a bereavement an employer should consider the requirement of the Equality Act 2010 to where reasonably practicable, to accommodate an employee's religion and beliefs when a death occurs.

Here's some customs that may require a bereaved employee to make arrangements that might be more than what might be expected. Remember individuals will have their own versions of these, so these are here only to give you an idea as to what might be asked of you with some popular religions.

In Islam burial should take place as soon after the death as is possible. This might mean that your employee needs emergency time off with little or no notice in order to facilitate a burial.

In Judaism, funerals must take place as soon as possible and on the same day as the death if this is practicable. The immediate family of the deceased must stay at home and mourn for 7 days. Following the death of his father or mother the observant male Jew is required to attend the synagogue to pray in the morning, afternoon and evening for 11 months of the Jewish calendar. Such a custom and tradition might mean the employee is taking emergency time off for dependents and making a flexible working request.

In Hinduism, close relatives will observe a 13-day period of mourning after the cremation. The closest male relative may want to take the ashes to the River Ganges in India. Such a custom and tradition might mean the employee is taking emergency time off for dependents and possibly requesting a short notice annual leave to travel with the ashes to India.

In Sikhism the cremation should take place as soon as possible after the death. Such a custom and tradition may mean the employee is taking emergency time off for dependents.

The biggest mistake an employer can make when a bereaved employee requests time off at short notice is to reject the request as 'out of hand'. Remember your most loyal, committed employees might one day request that you help and support them to honour their relative by them following the customs and traditions of their religion. Where the employer can support the employee at their time of bereavement, the employee will often be more loyal, and more committed following the death.

## What are contractual disciplinary, capability and grievance procedures?

This is where whoever drafted your contracts of employment has not included the phrase in relation to your Disciplinary, Capability and Grievance procedures, that these procedures are non-contractual.

We will frequently find when reviewing employment contracts that someone has added the entire disciplinary procedure within the main body of the contract or in the appendix and due to lack of words, has suggested that these procedures are contractual.

The danger of not following your own contracts, is that you as an employer could be sued for breach of contract. Not a pleasant thought, and something to be avoided if possible.

If you have non contractual disciplinary, capability and grievance procedures you get to choose whether you implement them.

This is a much preferable option than always having to follow your full disciplinary procedure because your procedure has been written as contractual.

## Can I anonymise witness statements?

When an employer identifies witnesses when investigating potential misconduct, it is normal for witnesses to either be interviewed or provide a statement that they sign and date. It is not uncommon for us to be asked whether the employer can anonymise witness statements obtained during the disciplinary investigation.

Whilst there is no legal requirement to disclose the identity of witnesses, failure to do so will always undermine the fairness of the process. This is because the accused employee has lost the right to challenge properly the evidence. Employers have an obligation to undertake a fair disciplinary procedure, which will include attempting to obtain reliable, corroborated evidence.

When a witness requests to remain anonymous, we believe that the employer's first step should explore the witness' reasons for wishing to remain anonymous. Perhaps they would prefer to remain anonymous. Perhaps they are unsure of what they have alleged. It is not unheard of for witnesses to fabricate allegations.

A common theme will be fear of retribution. If this fear is held and it is reasonable to anonymise the statement then it can be done, and a reasonable employer will seek further evidence to support the witness's statement.

This could be evidence of the Line Manager who interviewed the witness that wishes to remain anonymous. It could be that out of three witnesses one is unprepared to have their identity revealed but another two are comfortable.

A technique that can improve the fairness of an anonymised witness statement is where the investigating manager invites the employee to pose questions of the anonymous witness through the employer. The witness's answers can then be examined during the disciplinary process.

One final thing to note though. The employer should make the witness aware that their anonymity cannot be guaranteed. If the matter results in an employment tribunal, they may be subject to a witness order requiring their attendance at the employment tribunal to provide evidence. They will not be able to be anonymous them.

# What happens in a disciplinary hearing?

If it is decided that the matter will be resolved by calling a disciplinary hearing, then the employer must ensure that they follow their Disciplinary Policy. This will normally either live in the Policies and Procedures Manual or the Employee Handbook.

Employees who are requested (I prefer this to invited in my book you only get invited to parties!) to attend a hearing will receive a letter outlining the reason for the hearing, the allegations, evidence the employer will rely upon in the hearing and the right of accompaniment.

In the hearing the Chair will follow a structure rather than read a script, the structure being there to ensure no vital point is missed and that the hearing takes place in a fair and professional manner.

Hearings can be very difficult for both parties. There will undoubtedly be a lot of stress around. I believe that given we are trying to show that we treat people decently that this should be factored into the design of the hearing. Choose a venue that isn't a goldfish bowl. If possible, hold a hearing off site or at a different setting to the one your employee normally works at. Have a jug of water and glasses available. Bring some pads and pens in case they want to write a note and haven't got one with them. Sit around the corner of a table rather than behind the desk. Basically, treat people the way you would want to be treated and you would not go far wrong.

Once the hearing is concluded the Chair will ask the employee and their companion if they have anything that they would like to add, whether they feel they have had a fair hearing and whether they have any questions. Once the hearing is drawn to a close the Chair will explain what will happen next and how the employee can expect to receive communication from the employer as to the outcome of the hearing.

# Who can be an employee's companion to a disciplinary hearing?

The regulations state that an employee can be accompanied by a Trade Union Representative or a Work Colleague. Many employers have made the mistake of thinking that a) their employee isn't a member of a union so no need to include that one, or b) because we don't recognise a union for pay or collective bargaining this isn't applicable to them.

Employees can join any union or none. The days of a closed shop are well behind us. The employee may pay their membership fees by direct debit rather than any wage deduction the employer may be familiar with.

The Trade Union Representative may not be their regional representative but could be a TU rep who has been trained in matters of discipline and in the role of acting as a companion. I have seen shop stewards from the local factory accompany an employee who is a member of that union to a disciplinary hearing in a Day Nursery. All perfectly within the rules.

If in any doubt, ask the representative for their ID before commencing the hearing. No one who attends an Early Years or Childcare setting should be surprised to evidence who they are.

If you do not know who they are and they can't evidence that they are in fact a Trade Union Representative, you could choose to reschedule the hearing when they can be accompanied by someone who can evidence who they are or where it is a work colleague.

If a work colleague means it's their Dad, their Mum or worse still, their Uncle George who went on an ACAS course in 1979 then there is nothing you can do as its all within the regulations.

# When should you allow an employee to be accompanied by someone different?

The answer to this is probably whenever you wish, however it is worth noting that if you allow any companion without the process of considering the request and why you are permitting their chosen companion you will find it difficult to turn companions away. You will have set a precedent that in your organisation an employee can bring in any companion, that may or may not be a good idea.

One thing I would say is that in all my years in HR I have never known a situation go totally south because the employer allowed the employee to be accompanied by their companion of choice who wasn't a trade union representative or work colleague. What I do have is countless examples where work colleagues have behaved disgracefully and where trade union representatives have brought their union into disrepute.

A good Early Years and Childcare employer will consider allowing a companion who is not a trade union representative or work colleague in the following situations:

1. Where the employee would be at a disadvantage. For me this is often in the case of the micro-employer where there are perhaps 2 Directors and 1 employee and if the employee isn't given flexibility they cannot be accompanied.
2. Where an employee has a disability that means they will be at a disadvantage in the hearing and where the flexibility of companion will be a reasonable adjustment. Often where they have a physical impairment such as hearing loss where they would benefit from a sign language translator or where a brain injury would mean that they need a companion who is an advocate.

3. Where there is a language barrier. The employee whose English is not of a level where they can take part equally in the hearing, again this is where the employer hiring a translator to attend the hearing is a positive move to show they have conducted a fair hearing.
4. Where an employee's health is such that they are likely to be in a distressed state during the hearing. I have allowed husbands to attend grievance hearings with very upset employees before, just to ensure that the hearing takes place and that progress is made.

When it comes to companions, neutral companions who are friends rather than relatives will always be a preference. The issue I have seen with relatives is that their love for the employee can get in the way of them undertaking their role as effectively as possible. A friend or trusted ally is often better able to remain dispassionate and put across a strong argument in a professional and well-mannered fashion.

Employers should avoid having a solicitor attend with an employee. Case law has shown that it could be argued unfair to not allow legal representative to a manager or similar role in Early Years or Childcare if the outcome could be that this manager is barred from working with children. The case related to a teacher who was denied the right to legal representation at a dismissal hearing and the hearing subsequently led to them losing the ability to work as a teacher. This will be an issue in regulated professions such as education, health and social and childcare.

## What happens if they resign and go sick?

We frequently see employees resigning and then presenting a Statement of Fitness for Work to cover their period of notice. We are often asked whether the employer is liable to cover the cost of Statutory Sick Pay (SSP) for this employee (where they eligible) whilst they serve their notice from home. Almost always this is the case. There is no benefit to be gained by the employer starting the process to terminate the employee during their notice. We do recommend that if you are to introduce Company Sick Pay into your organisation that you consider whether you wish to state that Company Sick Pay will not be payable after an employee tenders their resignation.

## What if they resign with no notice?

This can happen in several circumstances, commonly it will be in response to:

1. Grievance. They are unhappy with something that has happened in the workplace and on submission of a grievance they resign with immediate effect. The risk of this to the employer is that the employee is considering now approaching the tribunal service to make a claim for constructive dismissal. An employee needs 2 years' service to bring a claim for constructive dismissal.

2. An investigation/disciplinary. They have been suspended, invited to attend a disciplinary hearing and in response to the employer's position they resign with immediate effect. This is often coupled with the line that this should not be seen as 'an admission of guilt'. Be careful if this occurs during an investigation into a safeguarding allegation as a resignation in those circumstances may not mean the automatic end of the process. Seek advice.
3. The new employer wants them to start immediately. We are seeing this more frequently in Early Years and Childcare. Sadly, some employers will suggest to their candidate to leave their current employer without any notice and to start immediately with them. If you feel like asking someone to do this, ask how you would feel if it was done to you.
4. Some form of trauma. Again, mental health is often cited as the reason why

an employee cannot work their notice and need to leave immediately. This can be work related or non-work related the net effect is the same, the employee refuses to return to serve their notice.
5. Heat of the moment. For example, an argument, incident, or situation that causes the employee to resign without any second thought. Let's take this a bit further.

She's walked…

From time to time, we get a call from a retained client that an employee has walked off the premises, often after an incident or what we technically describe in our office as 'a bit of a ding dong!'.

Whilst wherever this occurs this will be an issue, in Early Years and Childcare when an employee leaves the building before the conclusion of their shift is going to possibly put the Nursery out of ratio and leave children unsafeguarded.

This will therefore be serious misconduct on the part of the employee.

When we hear of these situations, we always ask the following:

- How long the employee has been employed?
- What do we know of the reasons behind the behaviour (ill health, stress, unresolved grievances etc?)
- How old is the employee? We do know that immaturity and other age-related circumstances can result in someone behaving in a way inconsistent with their responsibilities.

We ask this as Employment Tribunals have previously seen special circumstances from what others would see as unambiguous phrases like "I won't be back" and "I quit".

The tribunal has resolved that that management may have contributed to the employee's sudden resignation, perhaps an aggressive altercation with Nursery Owner, or an employee experiencing a period of extreme stress. In some circumstances the immediate acceptance of the heat of the moment resignation has led to a tribunal to conclude that an employee did not resign but was dismissed by the employer.

Sadly, sometimes when an employee leaves in the heat of the moment, we hear that the language was 'choice' and the doors may need new hinges.

We've also known for an employer to be shocked by the reckless driving and endangerment to car park users as the employee drove off at speed!

Not always does the employee add "You won't see me again, I'm done!". We've known them to clear their locker as they depart, suggestive of someone who is not intending to come back. Not even for their personal property.

With all this in mind what we want you to bear in mind is that despite what the employee may have said at the time, it could be dangerous for you to conclude that they meant what they said, "in the heat of the moment". A 'heat of the moment' resignation may mean that the contract has ended, but it may not.

If the employee has at least two years' continuous service with you, they could claim unfair dismissal at the employment tribunal. This would be them claiming constructive dismissal and that your actions have led to them leaving in this way.

The best response is to have a "cooling off" period and then, if possible, to contact the employee and establish whether they meant to resign and all the surrounding facts relating to the situation.

When this occurs, we don't want you to do or utter anything that could be interpreted by the employee as dismissing them. So unhelpful phrases like "don't bother coming back" or "if I see you again, I will fire you" should be avoided.

If an employee has left you under ratio or has left the premises during their shift in such a way as for you to feel there is a disciplinary case to answer, you must follow a fair procedure.

So, what do we mean by a cooling off period?

Well, if they storm off at Tuesday lunchtime, you would have thought that you would be hearing from them by Wednesday morning!

They may approach you by text, email or possibly call. We often find that employee's initial contact is nonverbal. Remember they may understand once delivered a resignation can't be unilaterally withdrawn by the employee. They may expect that you won't want to hear from them again.

If you do hear from them, and you want to and its best thing to do, them making contact after they have calmed down may mean you can work together to resolve the problem. If you want you can agree with the employee that he returns to work, without any break in his continuity of service.

## What if they don't contact you?

If you can't contact your employee, we tend to wait 24 to 48 hours to then write to the employee to acknowledge the without notice resignation and to confirm that they must return their uniform before you process them as a leaver.

If we aren't sure our letter will be steered towards the, we consider your actions to be resignation, if they are not, you must make contact by X …

What happens if they do turn up as if nothing happened?

The employee may well turn up for work the next day as if nothing happened, in that context we advise you investigate as normal and consider formal disciplinary action for the behaviour.

Remember if you accept their return and they have got a disciplinary case to answer if their actions were potentially gross misconduct (i.e., aggression, door slamming, car screeching) you should consider suspension pending the outcome of the investigation.

## Retirement

We used to have retirement as one of six potentially fair reasons for a dismissal. This was withdrawn in 2009 with the introduction of Age Discrimination Regulations. Retirement is now the name given for resignations by someone who has decided to leave employment. Not everyone will wait till when they can draw their pension. Increasing numbers of people over the age of 55 are leaving the labour market. We feel this represents a real opportunity for the Early Years and Childcare sector to offer roles to the recently retired 55-year-old. This is also known as the Great Return.

Employers need to be careful about asking their employees approaching retirement age about their plans for retirement. Under the Equality Act 2010. Whilst the act doesn't specifically state employers can't ask about someone's retirement plans, it is conceivable that an employer could be accused of age discrimination if they do.

This is because it would be discriminatory if it resulted in adverse treatment or decisions based solely on an employee's age. Treating employees differently or making assumptions about their abilities, commitment, or value to the organisation based on their retirement plans can be discriminatory.

Furthermore, there is stereotyping and bias. Asking about retirement plans may perpetuate stereotypes about older workers. If all employees nearing retirement age have the same plans or capabilities can be unfair and inaccurate. It may lead to biased decisions regarding promotions, training opportunities, or job assignments.

Finally, there is the risk of constructive dismissal. If an employer pressures or coerces an employee into disclosing their retirement plans, it may create an uncomfortable or hostile work environment. This can potentially amount to constructive dismissal, which occurs when an employer's actions make an employee feel forced to resign. An employee only needs 2 years' service to bring a claim for constructive dismissal.

## Redundancy

In the UK employers are obligated to follow strict procedures when carrying out compulsory redundancies in their Early Years and Childcare setting. Redundancy is a sensitive topic, and it can be a stressful and challenging time for employees, particularly when they are unsure about their rights and the procedures that their employer must follow.

As an employee facing compulsory redundancy, you have several rights that your employer must uphold. These rights include consultation, notice period, redundancy pay, any suitable alternative employment.

Firstly, consultation is a crucial part of the redundancy process, and your employer must consult with you before making any decisions. During the consultation, your employer should explain why the redundancy is necessary and provide you with an opportunity to express your views on the matter. Your employer should also discuss the possibility of avoiding the redundancy, such as by offering voluntary redundancy or reduced hours. The consultation process should be meaningful and take place in good time, allowing you to fully consider your options.

Secondly, your employer must provide you with a notice period before your employment comes to an end. The length of the notice period will depend on how long you have been employed with the business. For example, if you have worked for the business for between one and two years, you are entitled to one week's notice. If you have worked for the business for two years or more, you are entitled to a longer notice period. Your contract of employment should set out the notice period, and your employer must comply with this or provide a longer notice period.

Thirdly, you are entitled to receive redundancy pay if you have worked for the business for two years or more. The amount of redundancy pay you receive will depend on your length of service, your age, and your weekly pay. Your employer should provide you with a written statement setting out how they have calculated your redundancy pay. If your employer fails to provide you with the correct redundancy pay, you can take legal action against them.

Finally, your employer has a duty to look for suitable alternative employment for you if possible. This may involve offering you a different job within the business or providing you with information about job vacancies in other companies. Your employer must also consider any reasonable adjustments that may be necessary to enable you to take up alternative employment, such as providing training or adjusting your working hours. If your employer fails to consider suitable alternative employment, you may be able to claim unfair dismissal.

In summary, as an employee facing compulsory redundancy in a small business in the UK, you have several rights that your employer must uphold. Your employer must consult with you before making any decisions, provide you with a notice period, offer you redundancy pay, and look for suitable alternative employment for you. It is important to seek legal advice if you feel that your employer has not followed the correct procedures or has failed to provide you with your entitlements. The redundancy process can be a challenging time, but with the right support and understanding of your rights, you can ensure that you are treated fairly and lawfully.

## Transfer of Undertaking (Protection of Employment) Regulations aka TUPE

The Transfer of Undertakings (Protection of Employment) Regulations (TUPE) protects employees' rights when a business or undertaking is transferred to a new employer. TUPE applies when there is a "relevant transfer," which is a transfer of an economic entity that retains its identity after the transfer.

We see many TUPE transfers in Early Years and Childcare. Whether it be a pre-school being brought inhouse by the school it operates from, or the sale of a Day Nursery to another company.  The important fact to remember is that transfers don't just happen because something is bought or sold.

In the context of an out of school club operating from a school, if the school wants to bring the club in-house, it may trigger a TUPE transfer if the club is considered to be an economic entity that retains its identity after the transfer.

In this case, the employees of the out of school club would transfer to the new employer, in this case, the school, and their employment rights would be protected under TUPE.

The school would be required to inform and consult with the employees and their representatives about the transfer, and the employees would retain their existing terms and conditions of employment, including their continuity of service, pension rights, and collective agreements. The school would also be responsible for any outstanding liabilities, including any employment claims or liabilities arising from the pre-transfer period.

It's worth noting that not all transfers will trigger TUPE, and the specific circumstances of each case will need to be considered.

However, if TUPE does apply, it's important for both the outgoing and incoming employers to ensure that they comply with the regulations to avoid potential legal disputes and penalties.

Under the Transfer of Undertakings (Protection of Employment) Regulations (TUPE), an employer has an obligation to inform and consult with affected employees when a relevant transfer takes place. The purpose of the consultation is to ensure that employees are informed about the transfer, its implications for their employment, and any measures that the employer plans to take in relation to their employment.

The consultation process should begin in good time before the transfer takes place, and the employer should provide the affected employees with certain information in writing. This information should include:

1. The fact that a transfer is taking place, the reasons for it, and the date of the transfer.
2. The legal, economic, and social implications of the transfer for the affected employees.
3. Any measures that the employer plans to take in relation to the affected employees, such as changes to their terms and conditions of employment, and the reasons for those measures.
4. The number of agency workers employed, if any, and the parts of the business in which they are working.

5. The employer should also consult with any employee representatives, such as trade unions, if there are any. The consultation should be in good faith, and the employer should consider any representations made by the employee representatives.

It's important to note that the obligation to inform and consult with affected employees under TUPE applies to both the outgoing and incoming employers in a relevant transfer.

Where 20 of more employees will transfer this is known as collective consultation and requires the appointment of employee representatives for both the transferor and transferee to consult with on behalf of the employees.

Failure to comply with the obligation to inform and consult can result in legal action being taken against the employer, and the affected employees may be entitled to compensation.

# Providing Employee Liability Information in a Transfer

Under the regulations the outgoing employer (the transferor) is required to provide the new employer (the transferee) with certain information about the employees who will be transferred. This information sharing is allowed under UK GDPR. This will include information about any potential liabilities that the new employer may inherit because of the transfer such as accidents at work, grievances, disciplinaries, claims for unfair dismissal, discrimination, or breach of contract.

One area that is particularly important when we are talking about transfers between LA employers (schools) and the private sector will be Pension scheme liability.

Under TUPE, the outgoing employer is required to provide the transferee with a written information that sets out certain information about the employees who will be transferred. We recommend the transferee asks for completion of a table of information. This employee liability information must be provided at least 28 days before the transfer takes place. This is an improvement of the 14 days before transfer that used to be the rules.

We often see employers cite that they cannot share information before a transfer due to GDPR and we would argue that a transfer shouldn't go ahead unless you are satisfied with the information being shared. Don't rely on examples of Written Statements of Terms and Conditions, ask to see actuals.

Without good information, the transferee can't assess any potential risks associated with the transfer and take steps to mitigate those risks where possible. We will see transferors indemnifying the transferee which may include payments being held back to see what happens.

If the outgoing employer fails to provide the transferee with the required information about liability, the transferee may be entitled in a tribunal to receive compensation. We have had the case some years ago where the

Pre-school was that unhappy that they had lost the contract and it had been retendered that she produced fake contracts of employment for all staff with greatly increased hourly rates to try and 'price out the new provider'. It backfired when we pointed out that these fake contracts referred to the DBS before the DBS had been created and when the CRB was still in place. The Pre-school Owner had to admit they had asked their staff to sign the new contracts and to backdate these signatures.

## What happens with holidays when a TUPE occurs?

One of the common complaints we hear after a transfer of undertakings (TUPE) is finding out as a transferee (the incoming employer) that the transferor has transferred the staff with huge amounts of outstanding annual leave.

We would strongly advise that transferees insist as part of your due diligence that the transferor ensures that any accrued and untaken holiday has been given to the employees before transfer. This will by effect, will reduce your liability to pay out for holiday accrued when you did not operate the provision.

Holiday is paid at the rate of pay when it is paid/taken not when it was accrued. Therefore, this is particularly important when the transfer is after April 1st when the national minimum wage increases every year.

Employee Liability Information (ELI) which in a TUPE is shared no later than 28 days before a transfer does not need to include outstanding holiday entitlement but it is not a bad idea to ask about this.

Watch out for silliness such as...

Some transferors think they are being clever if they refuse to authorise holiday requests whilst the sale is going through, only for the incoming employer to be faced with the cost after the transfer.

Great record keeping is essential when it comes to holiday and finding out key members of your new team have been authorised to take leave at your busy time can also be a headache for transferees.

I've heard horror stories of employers who found that their Nursery Manager has been granted 2 weeks from the start of September by transferors in June, who then went on to sell their business on 31st August. No one would want their Nursery Manager out for the first two weeks of the business being transferred but as an employer it is hard to cancel an employee's leave request once authorised.

## How does a share sale differ from a TUPE transfer?

The Transfer of Undertakings (Protection of Employment) Regulations (TUPE) and share sales are two different legal concepts that have significant implications for businesses, including Day Nurseries, Pre-schools, and Out of School Clubs.

A share sale is a transaction in which the ownership of a company is transferred by selling its shares to a new owner. In this scenario the Ofsted registration may transfer if you are buying shares of a limited company. Unlike TUPE, which focuses on the transfer of employment contracts, a share sale involves the transfer of ownership and control of the entire company, including its assets, liabilities, and contracts, without automatically transferring the employment contracts of its employees. This means that in a share sale, the new owner acquires the business, including all employment contracts, and becomes the new employer of the employees.

The key difference between TUPE and a share sale is the automatic transfer of employment contracts under TUPE, which does not occur in a share sale. In a share sale, the employees remain employed by the same legal entity, and their employment contracts remain unchanged. However, the new owner of the shares acquires all the rights, benefits, and liabilities associated with the business, including any employment-related liabilities that may arise from the pre-existing contracts. This means that the new owner will need to comply with all applicable employment laws and regulations, including those related to employee rights, benefits, and protections.

Another important distinction between TUPE and a share sale is the level of control and involvement that the employees have in the transfer process. Under TUPE, employees have the right to be consulted about the transfer and can also object to the transfer if it would result in a substantial change to their working conditions. In contrast, in a share sale, employees do not have a direct say in the transfer process, as the transfer of ownership and control is negotiated between the existing and new owners.

In summary, TUPE and a share sale are two distinct legal concepts that have different implications for Day Nurseries, Pre-schools, and Out of School Clubs. TUPE focuses on the automatic transfer of employment contracts and provides employees with protections against unfair dismissal and the right to be consulted about the transfer. On the other hand, a share sale involves the transfer of ownership and control of the entire company, including all assets, liabilities, and contracts, without automatically transferring employment contracts. Understanding the differences between these two concepts is crucial for businesses in the early years education sector to ensure compliance with relevant employment laws and regulations during a transfer or sale process.

## Short Service

Where the employer decides to end the probationary period and at the same time support the employee to continue to improve their performance, then the employer would want to write to the employee outlining what this support will be and set some goals and deadlines.

What we tend to see where employment ends during or at the end of the probationary period is that the employer meets with the employee and explains that the performance has not met expectations and they are being terminated for non- completion of the probationary period. We would expect every employee to receive a written letter outlining that their employment has come to an end. In the case of pregnant employees, they have the right to receive a written reason for dismissal. Any dismissal in the probationary period of a pregnant employee would be considered a high-risk dismissal.

Finally, where an employer decides that a probationary period has been completed successfully, they will often write to the employee to outline that this has been successful. In some employers' salary is increased when an employee successfully completes a probationary period, or a colleague is entitled to a referral payment as the employee they referred has been successful.

Probationary periods are very useful devices for the employer to include in their Written Statement of Terms and Conditions. Since

April 2020 it is a requirement that where an employer chooses to use a probationary period, they have to state it in the Written Statement of Terms and Conditions. In the relevant clause (normally towards the top of the Written Statement of Terms and Conditions) they will explain the length of the probationary period and what will happen if performance does not meet the expectation of the employer during the probationary period for example, extend or terminate the employment during or at the end of the probationary period.

If an employer forgets to review the probationary period before the end of the expiration date, then it will be implied that the probationary period has been successfully completed.

There will be circumstances where in order to give a 'little wriggle room' employers have written into the Written Statement of Terms and Conditions that until the employer formally reviews the probationary period and communicates the outcome then probationary period is incomplete.

I am not an advocate of this approach as it relies on being reasonable. If a manager had annual leave and then some sickness absence and wanted to rely on not reviewing a probationary period until 6 weeks late, and the employee has been disadvantaged by this approach, would any termination due to non-completion of a probationary period be likely followed up by an appeal.

## So can I just write to her and dismiss?"

As HR Consultants we love this question. Often asked of us by an exasperated employer who has tried for weeks and months to get Employee A to do what they need them to do. As I have previously mentioned, these are not bad employers. They have tried to support the employee, done more than many employers would have done, yet still they find themselves asking the question, how can we bring this to an end?

In employment law we have 5 potentially fair reasons for a dismissal. We used to have 6, this was when retirement was compulsory with a set retirement age. These 5 reasons are:

1. Conduct
2. Capability
3. Redundancy
4. Statutory Reason (i.e., to carry on would break the law)
5. Some Other Substantial Reason.

The most common of these 5 reasons is Conduct. This is where the conduct of the employee is such to make dismissal a reasonable response by the employer. It can be because someone isn't performing the role they were employed to do. Sometimes we are unsure whether this can't do (capability) or won't do (conduct).

It is common for employers in Early Years and Childcare to want to explore whether they can dismiss an employee because of their poor attendance. This will be often treated as a conduct issue, as it's the employee's obligation when they took the job that they would attend work regularly.

In practice what we like to see is a process whereby the following has been met.

1. The employee has been made aware of the employer's expectations in terms of sickness absence reporting (usually in the Written Statement of Terms and Conditions and Employee Handbook).
2. The employer has explained to the employee their concern regarding their level of attendance and sought an improvement.
3. That where no improvement has occurred that the employee if to be dismissed, is dismissed with notice as per their Written Statement of Terms and Conditions.

Now the above assumes the employee is short serving and has no protected characteristics (more on them later in this book). We will often find that new employees to Early Years and Childcare have poor levels of attendance. Some of this can come from adapting to the many germs and viruses that travel through nurseries, particularly in September and January. We always say that employee's need to adjust to the battering their immune systems can receive. I can't personally think of another profession where there is a good chance a 'customer' will have wiped their nose on your clothes before lunchtime!

Let's break down those 3 stages. Why do we need to set out expectations in the first place. Well for one the worse thing anyone can ever say to you as an employer is "you never told me!". If you've assumed everyone will know that you report your absence in person on your first day of absence you won't have added this information to your sickness reporting procedure. An employee will therefore think that they do not need to let you know that they are not in work. They may have been able to text their last employer, so always establish what your expectations are.

In terms of the second stage, it can only be natural justice if the employee has been informed as to what is happening and what this could lead to. Many employees will need to be told that it's not OK to take time off work every time they aren't feeling 100%. In HR we feel this is getting worse, and a work ethic is not commonplace anymore. We recommend you still an employee down and explain your concerns over their attendance, making a note of the conversation so that, if required, you can refer to it in the future.

In the final stage, if an employer does decide to part company with the employee they should be treated with decency and paid their notice period. It is important for Early Years and Childcare employers to ensure that the statutory notice periods of 1 week for every year of service, up to a maximum of 12 weeks after 12 years' service is met. Employers can be more generous, but in my experience, it may not be money well spent.

We always recommend that the employer considers before any dismissal whether the employee has over 2 years' service, whether they have a claim for automatic unfair dismissal or whether they have a protected characteristic.

There are many factors that a HR or Employment Law consultant will consider when advising on a particular set of circumstances. Always seek advice before you make a costly mistake.

Finally remember, your Aunty Carol who once dated an Employment barrister and your business bestie on social media who owns a group of nurseries, may not be the best people to give you advice on whether you should dismiss someone for poor attendance.

Again, if I had a pound for every time, I had read the phrase of Facebook post; "Sack 'em", I would be very rich.

So, in answer to the question, can I just write to her and dismiss?

The answer is sometimes, yes.

Factors to consider will include the potential for the employee to attend the workplace in the next few days (i.e., have they been signed off sick), whether they have any protected characteristics and whether you have made your disciplinary and capability procedures contractual.

# Appendix

We are often asked what policies and procedures we should consider. Early Years and Childcare does LOVE a policy after all. Here's a comprehensive list of the employment policies you might want to consider for your organisation. Do note we don't recommend that you have these, but they are a list of policies.

Acas early conciliation policy
Accident investigation policy
Adoption leave
Adoption leave policy (adoption from overseas)
Adoption leave policy (adoption within UK)
Alcohol and drug testing policy
Alcohol or drug misuse policy
Anti-bribery policy
Anti-harassment and anti-bullying policy
Appearance and behaviour
Assistance dogs at work policy
Bereavement
Bonuses policy
Breastfeeding/expressing milk policy

Buying and selling holiday policy
Capability, disciplinary and grievance
Career breaks policy
Career planning policy
Carers
Company car policy
Compassionate leave policy
Compressed hours policy
Control of substances hazardous to health policy
Coronavirus and infectious disease
Coronavirus and return-to-work planning: Safe working policy
Coronavirus vaccination policy
Coronavirus workplace testing policy
Data protection
Data protection policy
Dealing with worker's death policy
Disciplinary procedure
Display screen equipment policy
Dispute resolution
Dress and appearance policy
Duvet day policy
Electing employee representatives' procedure (collective redundancy consultation)

Electing employee representatives procedure (informing and consulting on TUPE transfer)
Employee assistance programme policy
Employee of the month policy
Employee wellbeing
Employing reservists policy
Employing workers from overseas policy
Enhanced redundancy payments policy
Equal pay policy
Equality diversity and inclusion (EDI)
Equality, diversity and inclusion (EDI) policy
Equality, diversity and inclusion (EDI) statement (long form)
Equality, diversity and inclusion (EDI) statement (long form)
Equality, diversity and inclusion (EDI) statement for job advert (short form)
Expenses policy
Eye and eyesight testing policy
Family-friendly rights
Fertility treatment policy
First-aid policy
Flexible working
Flexible working requests policy
Flexitime policy
Giving references policy

Global anti-harassment and anti-bullying policy
Global flexible working policy
Grievance procedure
Hazard identification and risk assessment policy
Health and safety
Health and safety induction training policy
Health and safety policy statement
Health and wellbeing policy
Holiday and holiday pay
Holiday policy
Hybrid working policy.
Infectious diseases at work policy
International assignments policy
Jury service policy
Loans policy
Lone working policy
Long-service awards policy
Long-term internal secondment policy
Long-term sickness absence policy
Manual handling policy
Maternity leave
Maternity leave policy
Mediation policy
Menopause policy
Menstruation (period) policy

Mentoring policy
Mobile telephone use and driving policy.
Obtaining medical reports policy
Onboarding policy
Ordinary parental leave policy
Overtime and time off in lieu policy
Parental bereavement leave policy
Paternity leave
Paternity leave policy
Pay and benefits.
Pay review policy.
Payroll-giving policy
Performance improvement procedure
Permanent homeworking policy
Personal protective equipment policy
Personal relationships at work policy
Political activity at work policy
Pre-retirement training policy
Probation policy
Processing special category personal data and criminal records data policy
Protecting your business
Recruitment
Recruitment of people who have criminal record policy.
Recruitment policy
Recruitment referral bonus scheme policy

Redundancy
Redundancy policy
References
Religious holidays policy
Relocation assistance policy
Requests in relation to study or training policy
Retirement
Retirement policy (compulsory retirement age)
Retirement policy (no compulsory retirement age)
Sabbatical leave policy
Safe car travel policy
Safe overseas travel policy
Safeguarding: Recruiting people to work with children and/or vulnerable adults' policy
Second job policy
Secondment
Severe weather and disruptions to public transport policy
Shared parental leave.
Shared parental leave policy (adoption)
Shared parental leave policy (birth)
Shift-swap policy
Short-term internal secondment policy
Short-term sickness absence policy
Sickness and sick pay

Smoking policy
Specific events and incidents
Sporting events policy
Stop and search policy.
Supporting bereaved employees' policy
Supporting carers policy
Supporting employees experiencing pregnancy loss policy
Supporting employees with HIV and AIDS policy
Supporting foster carers policy
Supporting religious observance at work policy
Supporting staff experiencing domestic abuse policy
Technology and employee monitoring
Temporary homeworking policy during coronavirus pandemic
Time off for dependants' policy
Time off for domestic emergencies policy
Time off for employee representatives' policy
Time off for health and safety representatives' policy
Time off for medical and dental appointments policy

Time off for occupational pension scheme trustees policy
Time off for public duties policy
Time off for surgery policy
Time off for trade union learning representatives' policy
Time off work
Timekeeping policy
Trade union
Trade union derecognition procedure
Trade union recognition procedure
Training and development
Training and development policy
Transfer of undertakings
Transgender equality policy
Unauthorised absence policy
Use of agency workers policy
Use of CCTV policy
Use of company property policy
Use of email and internet at work policy
Use of hand-held or portable electronic devices policy
Use of mobile phones at work policy
Use of personal devices for work/bringing your own device to work policy
Use of social media policy
Variation of contract

Varying terms and conditions procedure
Vehicle tracking policy
Violence at work policy
Volunteer leave policy
Volunteering
Whistleblowing policy
Work equipment policy
Work experience policy
Working hours
Working hours policy
Work-related social events policy

# Checklist for Handling Grievances under ACAS Code of Practice

1. Has the matter been tried to be resolved informally, if not does the employee want the matter to be addressed formally using the Grievance Procedure?
2. Is the complaint about a manager? If so can another Manager investigate the complaint?
3. Has the employee put the grievance in writing?
4. Arrange a grievance hearing and send a standard letter to invite the employee to attend.
5. Hold the meeting in private without interruption from outside.
6. Arrange for someone to take notes with the Manager.
7. Check in advance of the hearing whether a grievance has been raised before and is it similar?
8. Remember a grievance hearing is nothing like a disciplinary hearing. Lay the room out to reflect this.

9. Make introductions for the benefits of all parties and the notes.
10. Outline how the hearing will be structured and everyone's role.
11. Make lots of eye contact with those speaking.
12. Make allowances for any letting off steam needed by the employee if they are under stress.
13. Ask the employee to restate their grievance.
14. Ask the employee how they would like to see the matter resolved.
15. Sum up the meeting at the end and possibly adjourn to investigate further.
16. Consider the use of a neutral mediator to sort out the grievance and maintain working relationships.
17. Tell the employee when they will receive a response to their grievance.
18. Explain that they will be given the right of appeal and point out that the right will be given in the written response.
19. Type up notes from meeting and place on personnel file swiftly after meeting.

20. Arrange the appeal swiftly if the employee appeals and organize for another Manager to hear the appeal if possible.
21. Always remain objective even if hearing an appeal about your own decision.
22. In cases involving a grievance about a fellow employee encourage use of the formal procedure or risk a constructive dismissal claim.
23. Talk privately with the employee about the concerns of fellow employees.
24. If this counselling does not resolve the issues, consider further action such as an independent mediator.
25. The meetings where the employee needs to be offered the right of accompaniment are the meetings where the employer deals with a complaint about 'a duty owed by the employer to the employee'. If in doubt offer accompaniment.

Another book by Imogen Edmunds, Chartered FCIPD

## How to Hire Superstars for your Day Nursery

This book aims to ask the reader the question what it takes to hire superstars. Those who we might other describe as those employees who 'get it' who will work well in a team and enhance your setting. This book is available from Amazon.

## About the Author

Imogen has worked in HR management since 1991. It was as a management trainee for Texas Homecare (you'll need to Google it if you are not of a certain age!) that she was first encouraged off the shop floor and into the offices to take on staff management.

In 2004 following the birth of her son 6 weeks earlier, Imogen decided to leave her corporate role and set up as an independent HR Consultant. She worked part time initially alongside caring for her son who went to Nursery at 5 months old. In fact, it was his first day at Nursery that Imogen discovered HR for Early Years and Childcare. She was invited into the office of the Day Nursery Owner to discuss their HR needs upon dropping off her son once they discovered she was a HR Consultant.

Now some 19 years on, Redwing is a team of 7. Imogen regularly speaks at Early Years and Nursery events across the country.

A note from the author: "It's a legal minefield out there! Having worked with Day Nurseries,

Pre-schools and Out of School Clubs across the country since 2004 I realised that they needed someone to call when things went South, and I don't mean to Hampshire! I also appreciated that Owners and Managers needed to sleep well at night and that they shouldn't be kept awake worrying about people management issues. Here at Redwing our clients get practical solutions from commercially minded, experienced HR Consultants who work with Day Nurseries, Pre-schools and Out of Schools all day, every day."

Imogen Edmunds

@imogenedmunds

info@redwing-solutions.co.uk
www.redwing-solutions.co.uk

01527 909436

To book a Discovery Call to find out how we can support your Early Years and Childcare setting with HR and Employment Law go to

Printed in Great Britain
by Amazon